THE
BEANIE BABY
HANDBOOK

By Les & Sue Fox

WEST HIGHLAND PUBLISHING COMPANY

AN "UNOFFICIAL" HANDBOOK

WEST HIGHLAND PUBLISHING CO., INC.
P.O. Box 36
Midland Park, New Jersey 07432

The photographs of the 99 piece Beanie Baby collection which appear on pages 26 to 124 (and elsewhere) represent the personal collection of Les and Sue Fox.

MANUFACTURED IN THE UNITED STATES OF AMERICA

Library of Congress Card Catalog Number: 97-90430

FIRST EDITION 10 9 8 7 5

ISBN 0-9646986-9-2

BEANIE BABIES™
ARE HERE TO STAY!

Forbes. C. 1996. Jeff Sciortino

H. Ty Warner, Ty, Inc., creator Of Beanie Babies

"A frenzy. The marketing score of the year."
Forbes, 10/21/96

"Warner is paddling hard to keep ahead of the tidal wave."
People Magazine, 7/1/96

"Beanies may become the biggest thing ever in retailing.
Elvis, Sinatra and The Beatles combined."
Richard Gernady, The Cat's Meow

"How many times can you buy something for five bucks
that's going to drive a kid bananas?"
James Weaver, U.P.S. Driver

"Beanie Babies are one of the hottest crazes to hit America."
Brad Bell, Sr. VP Marketing, McDonald's

ACKNOWLEDGEMENTS

The authors of THE BEANIE BABY HANDBOOK wish to express their sincere thanks to:

FORBES MAGAZINE
PEOPLE WEEKLY
THE BERGEN RECORD
WYCKOFF PUBLIC LIBRARY
MEDIA RELATIONS, McDONALD'S CORP.

PEGGY GALLAGHER
ANTIQUES & MORE
MAGGIE'S TOY BOX
DIANA LINKS
NANCY STEINFELD
JEANETTE LONG
JEFF SCIORTINO
GARY SAMUELS
HOLLY HAHN

The Bears Den
Bo-Ties
Mallory Brown
Stephanie Chernalis
Alix Cohen
Ben Cohen
Alexandra Long
Sam Chazen
Jamie Fox

And numerous other Beanie Baby dealers and aficionados who generously assisted us in our research and surveys

PROFESSIONAL PHOTOGRAPHY BY TRISH ELLIOTT
(Unless otherwise credited)
COVER DESIGN BY JAMES TICCHIO

Hi, Beanie Kids!!!

...and Beanie Moms & Dads, Too!

TM

KID BEANIE
Copyright 1997

Is Beanie Baby collecting the greatest hobby the world has ever known?

SOME PEOPLE THINK SO!

TABLE OF CONTENTS

PROFESSOR BEANIE'S

"Fairly Difficult"
<u>BEANIE BABY QUIZ</u>

T M

PROFESSOR
BEANIE
Copyright 1997

(Answers PAGE 128.)

****

(1) Which Beanie Baby mammal is an endangered species surviving in Florida?

(2) How many different Beanie Baby dogs have been whelped?

(3) What is the name of the Unicorn Beanie?

(4) Name the 4 domesticated Beanie Cats. (Hint: They rhyme.)

(5) Which two Beanie Babies are native to Australia?

(6) Only one Beanie Baby is not an animal. Who is it?

(7) What are the names of the 3 Beanie Babies with the American Flag sewn into their hides?

(8) Identify the 6 Beanies who celebrate birthdays in April.

(9) How many Beanie Babies were born in 1995?

(10) Which 8 Beanie Babies were clothed in tie-dyed fabric?

(11) Which Beanie's name is spelled the same backwards?

(12) List the 10 Teenie Beanie Babies given away with McDonald's Happy Meals. Which one was retired?

IF YOU WERE ABLE TO ANSWER ALL 12 QUESTIONS CORRECTLY (without cheating), GO EAT A BURRITO!

U.R.A. MAZED

HELP BEANIE THE PIRATE
Find His Lost Treasure

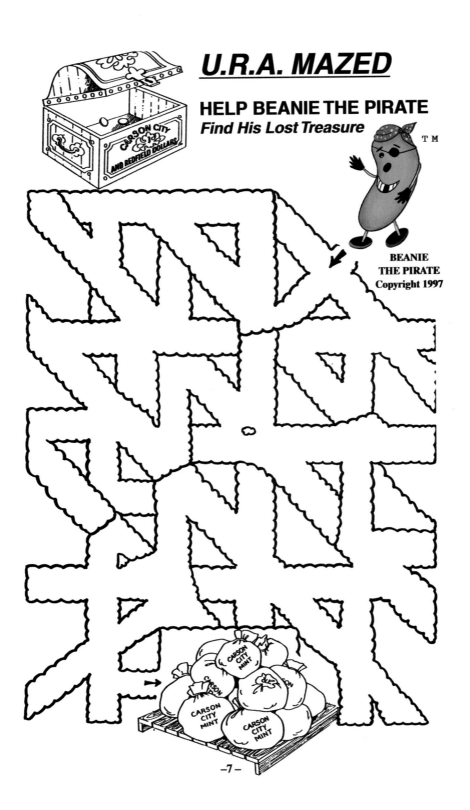

**BEANIE
THE PIRATE**
Copyright 1997

Look, it's
Benny Beanie's...

SECRET WORD PUZZLE!

(Find 44 Beanie names hidden by Beanie Bandito. Answer P. 128.)

B	E	W	C	R	E	X	R	E	H	T	I	L	S	S
B	N	I	P	A	R	T	O	R	A	T	E	D	D	Y
O	E	I	R	A	W	C	C	I	T	S	Y	M	A	F
N	Z	S	D	K	S	Y	S	A	Y	K	N	I	I	F
G	L	A	S	A	T	R	P	P	O	L	Y	S	S	O
O	R	U	B	I	E	S	P	O	T	E	E	C	Y	N
M	T	A	P	K	E	A	P	U	T	F	R	O	B	I
E	T	P	C	L	H	S	N	O	R	T	H	O	O	T
L	I	A	E	I	S	A	L	L	Y	Y	P	P	D	N
H	U	G	Y	D	E	E	P	S	E	A	M	O	R	E
Q	S	N	I	P	E	K	I	N	G	N	U	T	S	L
P	I	L	F	E	T	A	L	O	C	O	H	C	U	A
O	G	A	R	C	I	A	S	E	L	B	B	U	B	V

A PERSONAL MESSAGE FROM THE AUTHORS

Collecting is in our blood. You name it, we collect it.

In 1957, Les Fox was a typical sixth grader living in Queens Village, New York. After school, he pushed tarnished Lincoln pennies into slots in a blue cardboard album. Over the years, the disease has spread. Beanie Baby collectors Les and Sue have come a long way, baby, in their incurable addiction!

By 1974, we were operating a shop in Manhattan's Antique Center of America, while co-managing the Rockefeller Center numismatic showroom of Perera Fifth Avenue.

On August 15, 1977, the day before Elvis died, we published the first edition of "Silver Dollar Fortune-Telling." The book contained the "crazy" prediction that mint condition coins, then worth as little as $10-$20, were destined to appreciate to $100's and $1,000's. This actually happened during the inflationary 1980's. Over the next ten years, our book sold more than 120,000 copies!

In 1987, we set two record prices at Sotheby's art auctions, first for a 1924 seascape by American Impressionist Reynolds Beal, then for a 1975 primitive oil by 90 year-old American folk artist Mattie Lou O'Kelley of Georgia.

On October 5, 1988, we ended our rare coin career with a bang at the fabulous Plaza Hotel. Working with a group of 75 collectors, we auctioned an amazing group of United States gold coins. Most possessed famous pedigrees. The average lot in the multi-million dollar sale realized $20,000!

In 1991, the year we were blessed with the birth of our daughter, Jamie, we acquired America's finest Cigar Store Indian, whom we named "Princess Lottabucks." We've since sold this piece, but we still own "Abner," a museum quality American folk art rooster we purchased about the same time.

We also began collecting Steiff teddy bears in 1991, when a 1926 "Anniversary" bear fetched $88,000 at auction. We didn't buy that one. Instead, we later settled for a pair of Limited Edition reproductions at $500 apiece. In 1994, we sold our prized 1907 American Pairpoint Apple Tree Lamp at Sotheby's to help finance the renovation of our home. We've "collected" a total of 17 houses since 1975.

Among the things we collect: French Cameo Glass, carousel horses, 19th Century painted furniture, vintage photos and Daguerrotypes, old toys, antique birdhouses, butter churns, coffee grinders, children's chairs, 1950's rock 'n' roll records, Queen Victoria mementoes, antique American school items, early Coca Cola and advertising collectibles (we've sold two collections at auction), quilts, pharmacy tins, McDonald's memorabilia, and hand-painted wooden signs.

So why on earth are we now collecting Beanie Babies?

Well, actually, our six year-old got us started. Typical, right? Like millions of kids across America, Jamie simply wanted "one." At $5, how could we say no? Sure. Buy a Beanie Baby. It's cute, it's well made, it's cuddly, and...Hey, look! There's a heart-shaped card attached to the toy with the animal's name, birthday, and a poem. Clever. What'll they think of next? Well, how about 100 different Beanie Babies and counting! And we can't wait for the new ones!

At Jamie's last birthday party we handed out 25 Beanies as favors and -my goodness - everyone in town is still talking about it, since some of the freebees have been retired!

Bottom line? We soon decided we had to have them all. The complete collection in this book is ours. That's what happens when the illness strikes.

Does the Beanie Baby phenomenon surprise us? Not really. Look at Barbie Dolls. How many of those things can one little girl own? (Answer: A lot.) Are Beanies, which appeal to both sexes, a passing fad? Maybe, but we don't think so. They're too catchy, and too affordable. And some, like Kiwi, Chops and Wrinkles, are fabric-sculpted works of art. Like they say, it ain't over until the fat Beanie sings!

LES AND SUE FOX
WYCKOFF, NEW JERSEY

STOP THE PRESSES!

BEANIE BABY BULLETIN

As announced by Ty, Inc., on Mother's Day (Sunday, May 11, 1997), the following last-minute information supercedes the pages ahead.

NEWLY *RELEASED* BEANIE BABIES

Baldie/Eagle	Dottie/Dalmation	Pugsley/Pug
Blizzard/Tiger	Echo/Dolphin	Roary/Lion
Chip/Calico Cat	Jolly/Walrus	Toughy/Terrier
Claude/Crab*	Nanook/Husky	Waves/Whale
Doodle/Rooster*	Peace/Bear	*(Tie-dyed)

NEWLY *RETIRED* BEANIE BABIES

Bubbles	Flash	Grunt	Radar	Splash
Digger	Garcia	Manny	Sparky	

(All now "Highly Recommended" at $10–$20 up!)

Full-Page Color Photos of all new Beanie Babies will appear in next year's BEANIE BABY HANDBOOK.

Jenna (designer of "Spooky") and Lauren Boldebuck, and cousin Cole Michel, frolic in Ty Warner's "posh" Oak Brook pad surrounded by plush Beanie Babies.

Entrepreneur Ty Warner, who graduated Kalamazoo College in 1962, relaxes with his real life Nip the Cat, Nokomis.

THE BEANIE BABY STORY

Have you read today's Beanie Baby column in your local newspaper? Special features telling how kids got started collecting are springing up all over the country. Like Brittany Kirk, 6, of Rivervale, New Jersey, who received some Beanies from a friend in Chicago. After Brittany's grandmother in Louisville, Kentucky continued to send more for birthdays and holidays, the kindergartner was hooked. She now has 60 Beanie Babies. "Kids bring them to school for nap time," she revealed. "And a lot of parents use them for rewards."

On the Internet, "Beanie Hunter" stories are more intriguing. People regularly report on how they've snared valuable "retired" Beanies browsing in obscure gift shops (hospital and airport shops often contain hidden treasures.) While some have sold for windfalls, most have decided to hang on, or to trade for Beanies they "need."

Forbes Magazine calls it "Mystique Marketing."
Kids call it fun!

Whatever you want to call it, the Beanie Baby story is the real life version of the obsession with a "Turbo Man" toy, last holiday season's wacky Arnold Schwarzenegger adventure film. ("Jingle All The Way.") Here's how it all began.

Take one Ty Warner, 57, who quit Dakin toys in 1980 to "goof off" in Italy for a few years (his own words), mix in some funky, understuffed animals, price them for the elementary school crowd, and—voila—success!

Sounds simple, doesn't it? Okay, then why didn't *you* think of it? Same reason you didn't invent the safety pin or Microsoft. Somebody at least as smart as you thought of it first! Well, like they say, the world will beat a door to the man (or woman) who invents the better mouse trap. And that's just what happened with Beanie Babies.

Plush toys, or toys wrapped in soft, velvety material, have been around forever. So it didn't exactly take a genius to realize that such things can sell like hotcakes. After all, according to *Teddy Bear Review*, there are an estimated 3,000,000 teddy bear collectors in America. However, it did take a genius to figure out how to sell 200 million bundles of plastic beans sewn into the shapes of bears, foxes, ladybugs, tigers and kangaroos to *10 million kids!*

The Beanie Baby King handles a shipment of Ty's toys.

Meet Ty Warner, the man who beat you to it.

Mr. Warner is a very private person. He endures seeing his picture in magazines and newspapers because he loves making toys, and making kids happy. Everyone we spoke to says the same thing about the man: He's a charming gentleman. People Magazine reports that he lives with his companion, Faith McGowan, a former lighting store manager, and her daughters, Lauren Boldebuck, 14, and sister Jenna, 12, in a "posh" home in Oak Brook, Illinois. Oak Brook just happens to be the national headquarters of McDonald's.

As legend has it, the Beanie Baby concept was hatched in 1992 and developed in 1993. "Spot The Dog" kicked off the ruckus. Spot was born on January 3, 1993 and is still alive and well, meaning: he has not yet been "retired." Three days later his cousin "Patti The Platypus" was introduced to humanity, and two weeks hence along came "Bones The Dog."

The rest is history.

But how did Ty Warner *know* that the 1990's was the right time and place for Beanie Babies? After all, he has stated flatly: "I knew I had a winner." And what makes him think that the trend is not about to end? Plush "trolls" were *the* toy fad of 1991 and 1992, and where are they now?

The difference, we think, is that Beanie Babies are far superior. No offense, but trolls don't quite stir the imagination the way tamed wild beasts do. Not to mention the fact that trolls are, well, ugly! Sorry to all you troll collectors out there, but we just don't see kids forming permanent attachments to smiling Teutonic cave-dwellers the way they do to Spot, Patti or Bones. Or Stinky The Skunk for that matter.

The idea of enticing children to love "baby" animals is nothing new. Sesame Street's Muppets spawned Muppet Babies and most of Disney's characters have offspring. But there is something indefinably "special" about Warner's menagerie. The word "cute" doesn't quite explain it.

Getting back to Forbes' "mystique marketing" theory, the Beanie Baby "craze" has obviously been fueled by a clever business strategy. Ty, Inc., a privately held company with no plans to go public (they told us) has relied on good old fashioned supply and demand to sweep America off its feet. For the first year or two, the toys were promoted extensively, but there were no lines around the block. Only a fraction of today's estimated 40,000 outlets (mostly small gift and card shops, and toy stores) were anxious to handle the merchandise, which didn't start jumping off the shelves until mid-1996. Then, without warning, Lefty The Donkey and Righty The Elephant (Democrats and Republicans) sold out at toy fairs in Chicago and San Diego. Word spread of the excitement, and retailers began ordering larger quantities of the line.

As if lured by the Pied Piper, more kids began to take notice of the "cute babies." First girls, but almost immediately boys, too, thanks to such manly Beanies as Crunch the Shark and

Radar the Bat, decidedly not for the squeamish.
And that's when the shortages arose.

Ty Warner decided initially not to supply the big national chains, notably Toys "R" Us. (He does supply smaller chains like Noodle Kidoodle.) This was a wise move, since a $5 product doesn't need to be discounted and the big boys can sometimes be too controlling. "If we were to sell to Wal-Mart," says Warner, "we would not be paid in 30 days." Thus, because of both surging demand and production delays, Beanie Baby sellers found themselves in a strange predicament. Customers were chomping at the bit ("I need Freckles today!") but the product flow had ceased.

You'll never guess what happened next.
It is common knowledge that people always want what they can't have. If the Ty company says they're temporarily out of stock, what's the solution? Order extra! Except for one slight problem. *Everyone wants extra!* Including McDonald's, who temptingly offered to buy 300 million "mini" Beanie Babies. (Sold out!) In late 1996, Nordstrom's department stores convinced Warner to let them jump on the bandwagon. Two million Beanie Babies later, Nordstrom's is still riding the wave, as some critical Warner-watchers ask themselves what happened to Mr. W's promise to remain exclusive to his mom and pop customers, and not to make any licensing deals.

Frankly, this whole thing has gotten a little out of hand (a little?) and needs to get back on an even keel, which should start happening in 1998. We do not fault Ty Warner for any of his business decisions. In his position, I'm sure most of us would have acted similarly. In fact, by "creating empty shelves" (in economics, it's called demand exceeding supply), a manufacturer opens the doors to his competitors. This has actually happened, with the emergence of Wal-Mart's $3.99 Pebble Pets (Imperial Toy Corp.) and other substitutes grabbing a modest market share. Most kids, however, know the difference, and prefer the "cachet" of the Beanie Baby name tag. In other words, they'll wait for the real McCoy.

Hey, give the man credit! Sure he's made a fortune, but a year ago April, Warner leased three 737's to fly Beanies from Seoul, Korea to U.S. stores in time for Easter. He "retires" six surprise Beanies twice a year (end of June and December), replacing them with colorful new family members, which adds to the thrill. And he actively promotes Beanies on the Internet (TY.COM) which serves all concerned.

* * * * * * * * * * * *

There are a thousand reasons for Beanie Babies to die out, as fads usually do. But we agree with Ty Warner's philosophy. Kids, especially those from Kindergarten to sixth grade, have never had a *nationally recognized* collector's item before. So, if there is one reason in that thousand for Beanie Babies to thrive and prosper, here it is: No one has yet invented their successor.

Until that day, expect mob scenes at toy stores to continue, and more "911" calls like the one made recently in Springfield, Illinois: "Help! We're being attacked by Beanie Baby collectors!"

People Weekly. C. 1996. Kevin Horan.

A GUIDE TO COLLECTING
BEANIE BABIES

Introduction

Collectors (to paraphrase comic Steve Martin) are a "wild and crazy" breed. They will fill their entire house with treasures, also known as "junk." They'll think nothing of showing up an hour early, in the pouring rain, for a tag sale which "starts promptly at 9 a.m., no early birds" hoping for a bargain. Yes, every once in a while some lucky duck discovers an 18th Century duplicate of the Declaration of Independence behind a framed picture - and auctions it for $2.4 million! (True story!) However, the usual "find" is more on the order of a $3.50 Roseville Vase, the common 1930's orange and green Peony style, with a slight edge chip, value if perfect $40.

It matters not that such quests for gold generally end in disappointment. To the true collector, that million dollar "strike" is just around the corner. Everyone knows someone whose cousin Emily accidentally sold her original Barbie Doll, or her grandmother's autographed first edition of Moby Dick, for a dollar. It therefore follows that a determined collector, armed with a pocketful of cash, will sooner or later stumble across a bonanza.

In thirty plus years of diligent, serious collecting, it's never happened to us. And it probably never will. The best we've ever done has been to make sound purchases of the finest quality antiques or collectibles we can afford, and to hold on for as long as possible. The old axiom is true: A serious collector makes the best investor.

So our first piece of advice to Beanie Baby collectors is the same tip we give everyone else. Buy what you like, study the hobby, and shop carefully.

As we go to press with the first edition of this book (May, 1997) the Beanie Baby craze has mounted to a fever pitch. While some are content to wait for the next shipment of Beanies to arrive at their local gift, toy or Teddy Bear shop at $5.00 (if the UPS truck isn't hijacked), Internet surfers are regularly trading common Beanies (yes, many Beanies *are* decidedly common, made in the millions and not yet scarce in mint condition) at $10 to $25. Over the long term we sincerely believe the value of Beanie Babies is destined to rise. If you collect wisely and well, your collection will treat you right.

WHICH BEANIES ARE "THE BEST"?

We've been following the chit-chat on the W.W.W.'s three most active Web sites: *TY.COM, BEANIE MOM and BEANIE BABY.* ("Beanie Mom" is Sara Nelson of Virginia.) Increasingly, collectors are asking each other which Beanie Baby is "the best."

Over time, surveys will undoubtedly indicate different Beanies winning popularity contests. Just for fun, we have decided to list what we think are the 10 most popular Beanie Babies (at the moment) as well as the 10 rarest. Keep in mind that tastes change. And from a rarity point-of-view, it is possible that some of today's *least* popular styles could turn out to be among the most desirable from an investment aspect.

The 10 Rarest BEANIE BABIES

		1997 Value
1.	SPOT (Without spot)	$1,200
2.	PEANUT (Dark blue)	1,500
3.	QUACKERS (No wings)	1,000
4.	ZIP (All black)	1,000
5.	PATTI (Maroon)	750
6.	CHILLY	750
7.	NIP (All gold)	750
8	HUMPHREY	650
9.	PEKING	500
10.	TEDDY (Special colors)	200 up

In the pages ahead, the authors have made a concerted effort to estimate the *actual production figure* of every Beanie Baby produced since 1993. These figures are based on collector and dealer surveys and an extrapolation of Ty, Inc.'s reported gross sales. Based on an average distribution price of $2, we believe that more than 160 million toys have been manufactured to date. (Not including the McDonald's Teenie Beanies, estimated at an additional 300 million toys spread over 21,000 McDonald's worldwide.)

Photo courtesy McDonald's Corp. The Teenie Beanie Baby Collection.
According to Business Week, more popular than food!

Despite our mathematical acumen, the fact remains that some or all of our estimated production figures may be wrong. We have no doubt that other "experts" will attempt to correct our statistics, which is all for the good since the Ty company does not presently wish to divulge the quantities of Beanie Babies produced. Keep in mind, however, that without such official information there is no way to really know how many Beanies exist. Each person has seen only his or her share of the total population and has absolutely no way to verify whether the observed relative rarity is meaningful. By surveying a large number of observers, we feel that we have presented a *significantly* more accurate overview.

Should a hoard of 5,000 Humphrey The Camels turn up tomorrow, we would be extremely surprised. But such an event is far from impossible. Our statistics are not guaranteed!

Where we indicate production figures as "Total Made," we are of course referring to total made *to date*. In the case of retired Beanies, these figures are final. In the case of active sellers, we have no way of knowing how many more will be made, although we do offer an educated guess as to when current Beanies might be retired.

The 10 Most Popular BEANIE BABIES

1. GARCIA
2. STRIPES
3. FRECKLES
4. WRINKLES
5. SPARKY
6. BONGO
7. POUCH
8. CHOCOLATE
9. LIZZY
10. NUTS

(TO OUR READERS: Don't get mad if your favorite Beanie isn't on the above list. The results of popularity contests are subject to change.)

ARE BEANIE BABIES "COLLECTIBLE?"

A headline earlier in this book flashes the message: "Beanie Babies Are Here To Stay!" But are they, really? Can such a *mass produced item* survive the test of time? Remember, between 1 and 2 million examples of the *average* Beanie were made (the same as many Barbie dolls.) Some say these toys are merely disposable novelties. Which may be true. Within a decade, and possibly a lot sooner, "survivors" will be relegated to storage boxes in attics and basements, if not the garbage can. Among the warnings of obsolescence we've heard is that over the years fabric simply "disintegrates," sealing the long term fate of new friends like Chocolate and Wrinkles.

Such dire predictions are music to the ears of true collectors, including the authors. Even if it were a fact that fabric self-destructs (this is nonsense - look at antique dolls and quilts), the good news is: Whoever manages to preserve and protect their Beanie Babies will have a genuine prize. Most of today's "readily available," modestly priced Beanies will *not* be properly cared for. Thus, when aging kids get serious about owning a *collection* of the miniature plush animals, they're going to wonder what happened to all the mint condition specimens with perfect noses and crisp, heart-shaped tags.

And that's when the collectibility of Beanies will be widely acknowledged. A replacement of Chocolate in flawless condition currently costs $5. In a few years, the price will be $10. In 10 years, when millions of Chocolates have disappeared, a superb example could easily run $40 to $50. While this may seem preposterous in 1997, that's the way it always works with collector's items. First they're abundant, then they're not. In 1976, the authors stashed away 200 McDonald's yellow and white plastic "garbage can banks" at 15 cents apiece. Two decades later they're worth five bucks a pop!

It's our own personal "theory of scarcity" that at least 90% of *almost everything* gets lost, stolen or destroyed within 10 years. (Sometimes it only takes *10 seconds* to lose your keys!) Why should Beanies defy the laws of human nature? Yes, right now lots of people are stashing away extra Beanies as an investment. However, most will lose patience and bail out within a few years. Already, many owners of the retired Beanies are parting with their treasures for a quick profit. And we don't blame them. Selling a $5 toy for $50-$250 in two or three years is sound business. The point is, only a tiny percentage of Beanies will be sealed in Zip-Loc bags and treated with TLC until the year 2007, no matter how well-intentioned their owners. Fires, floods, accidents and *life itself* will simply take its toll. Whoever is lucky (and smart) enough to hang on to some top grade Beanie Babies for the long haul will be the future supplier to tomorrow's collectors.

BEANIES VS.BARBIES

Are Barbie Dolls collectible? They, too, were mass produced. Even Barbie's most expensive recent release, *Pink Splendor,* was issued in a "limited edition" of 10,000 pieces and priced at $900! (You'd better believe 9,999 of those will be saved in the airtight box!)

According to Barbie expert Jane Sarasohn-Kahn of Toy Trader magazine, the entry-level $5 Barbie (known as the "hair play doll") does not compare to the $5 Beanie.

"You have to spend $20 on a Barbie to get the same play value as a $5 Beanie Baby," Ms. Kahn told us. "Mattel is concerned about this new phenomenon eating into their sales."

Not to worry. Mattel, who is in the process of acquiring Tyco Toys (a different company than Ty, Inc.) still sells more than a billion dollars a year in Barbie Dolls, a "fad" some expected to end 30 years ago! This year, the *one-billionth* Barbie will come off the production line. And it's certainly not over, as long as new customers keep being wrapped in pink blankets!

After speaking to Ms. Kahn, we easily convinced her that Beanie Babies have other advantages over Barbies. They appeal to both sexes, and they're more diverse. *Plus*, their individualized birthdays and poems set them apart from all other toys. Kids love having a toy with the same birthday as theirs. (Watch for more Beanie Baby "accessories.")

THE FUTURE OF BEANIE BABIES

As we've stated, Beanie Babies will be around for years to come. Their rarity will increase down the line, and so will their popularity as more and more adults start a collection. (It's easy, just ask us!) Next: "Beanie Babies: The Movie"?

As to the large supply of Beanies, don't forget there is also a large demand. Without demand, a small supply is meaningless. That's why, believe it or not, scarce 20th century Lincoln pennies, or a 1917 Steiff black bear (1,700 made, value $50,000), can be more valuable than ancient Greek and Roman coins, or unpopular one-of-a-kind antiques.

Do we expect common Beanie Babies to climb from $5 to thousands? Absolutely not. It's possible they will remain at $5 forever. But we doubt it. They have too much going for them. So take good care of your Beanies, don't cut off their tags and think about buying some of the *rare ones* now!

Introducing . . .

THE BEANIE BABY
COLLECTION
Of Les, Sue and Jamie Fox

ALLY
(The Alligator)

TOTAL MADE:	**3,000,000**	**Birthday: 3-14-94**
(Est.) Survival 2007:	**300,000**	*Likely to be retired:* **1998**

ISSUE PRICE:	**$5.00**
1997 Value	**5.00**
(Est.) Year 2007	**40.00**

 **RECOMMENDED**   ✈ *ADD 10% TO 20% PREMIUM FOR FLAWLESS CONDITION WITH TAG*

BEANIE HUNTER'S TIPS: Ally the Alligator was the very first Beanie Baby purchased by the authors' daughter. Among the most common of the group, Ally is treated with dignity and tender loving care. But kids are kids, so we have a spare!

✺ __BERNIE__ ✺

(The St. Bernard)

TOTAL MADE:	1,000,000	Birthday: 10-3-96
(Est.) Survival 2007:	100,000	*Likely to be retired:* __2000__

ISSUE PRICE:	**$5.00**
1997 Value	**5.00**
(Est.) Year 2007	**40.00**

 RECOMMENDED ✈ *ADD 10% TO 20% PREMIUM FOR FLAWLESS CONDITION WITH TAG*

__BEANIE HUNTER'S TIPS:__ One of the newest Beanie Baby dogs. Bernie's no Beethoven look-alike but he doesn't slobber in your slippers either. Unlike Spot, no rare variety of this winsome canine has accompanied his debut.

☼ **BESSIE** ☼
(The Brown and White Cow)

TOTAL MADE:	2,000,000	Birthday: 6-27-95
(Est.) Survival 2007:	200,000	*Likely to be retired:* **1999**

ISSUE PRICE:	$5.00
1997 Value	5.00
(Est.) Year 2007	40.00

 RECOMMENDED   ✈ *ADD 10% TO 20% PREMIUM FOR*
FLAWLESS CONDITION WITH TAG

BEANIE HUNTER'S TIPS: There are two cows (and two bulls) in the Beanie Baby farm collection. We predict that a black bull named Ferdinand and a blue cow named Bluebelle will be introduced into the line by the time Bessie retires in two years.

☼ <u>BLACKIE</u> ☼

(The Black Bear)

TOTAL MADE:	3,000,000	Birthday: 7-15-94
(Est.) Survival 2007:	300,000	*Likely to be retired:* <u>**1997**</u>

ISSUE PRICE:	**$5.00**
1997 Value	**5.00**
(Est.) Year 2007	**40.00**

 **HIGHLY RECOMMENDED**

✈ *ADD 10% TO 20% PREMIUM FOR FLAWLESS CONDITION WITH TAG*

<u>BEANIE HUNTER'S TIPS:</u> Blackie is still reasonably priced and should be added to your collection quickly. In his prone position, Blackie has been mistaken for a bearskin rug, so tread carefully.

☼ **BONES** ☼
(The Dog)

TOTAL MADE:	**4,000,000**	**Birthday: 1-18-94**	
(Est.) Survival 2007:	**400,000**	*Likely to be retired:* **1997**	

ISSUE PRICE:	**$5.00**
1997 Value	**5.00**
(Est.) Year 2007	**40.00**

 **RECOMMENDED**   ✈ *ADD 10% TO 20% PREMIUM FOR*
FLAWLESS CONDITION WITH TAG

BEANIE HUNTER'S TIPS: Although bones and Rover both look like Snoopy, Bones has larger eyes and a round-stitched snoot.

☼ **BONGO** ☼
(The Monkey)

TOTAL MADE:	3,000,000	Birthday: 8-17-95
(Est.) Survival 2007:	300,000	*Likely to be retired:* **1997**

ISSUE PRICE:	$5.00
1997 Value	5.00
(Est.) Year 2007	50.00

 RECOMMENDED 　　　✈*ADD 10% TO 20% PREMIUM FOR*
FLAWLESS CONDITION WITH TAG

BEANIE HUNTER'S TIPS: Bongo was originally called "Nana" when distributed in late 1995. He was manufactured with two different tails, one light and the other dark. The relative rarity of the tails is presently unknown but the discontinued dark tail is scarcer.

☼ <u>BRONTY</u> ☼
(The Brontosaurus)

TOTAL MADE:	100,000	Birthday: 1995
(Est.) Survival 2007:	10,000	*RETIRED:* <u>June, 1996</u>

ISSUE PRICE:	**$5.00**
1997 Value	**200.00**
(Est.) Year 2007	**1,000.00**

 **HIGHLY
RECOMMENDED**

✈ *ADD 50% TO 100% PREMIUM FOR
FLAWLESS CONDITION WITH TAG*

BEANIE HUNTER'S TIPS: Bronty is considered the rarest of the three dinosaurs. Handle with care as his seams are fragile. While the two plant eaters, and the carnivore, are currently extinct, we expect to see three replacements hit the market by 1998.

☼ BUBBLES ☼
(The Fish)

TOTAL MADE:	1,000,000	Birthday: 7-2-95
(Est.) Survival 2007:	100,000	*Likely to be retired:* __1997__

ISSUE PRICE:	**$5.00**
1997 Value	**10.00**
(Est.) Year 2007	**75.00**

 HIGHLY
RECOMMENDED

✈*ADD 25% TO 50% PREMIUM FOR*
FLAWLESS CONDITION WITH TAG

BEANIE HUNTER'S TIPS: Bubbles is likely to be retired soon. This fishy collector's item is still very affordable, especially if you can find one at $5. Bubbles' fabric appears to be an exact match to Bumble the Bee.

☼ BUCKY ☼

(The Beaver)

TOTAL MADE:	1,000,000	Birthday: 6-8-95
(Est.) Survival 2007:	100,000	*Likely to be retired:* **2000**

ISSUE PRICE:	$5.00
1997 Value	5.00
(Est.) Year 2007	40.00

 RECOMMENDED ✈ *ADD 10% TO 20% PREMIUM FOR FLAWLESS CONDITION WITH TAG*

BEANIE HUNTER'S TIPS: Bucky is a Beanie Baby you can really sink your teeth into. Since no similar animal would remain if Bucky retired, this beaver's dam is probably watertight for a few years.

☼ <u>BUMBLE</u> ☼

(The Bee)

TOTAL MADE:	75,000	Birthday: 1995
(Est.) Survival 2007:	7,500	*Retired:* <u>June, 1996</u>

ISSUE PRICE:	$5.00
1997 Value	150.00
(Est.) Year 2007	900.00

 **VERY HIGHLY
RECOMMENDED**

✈ *ADD 50% TO 100% PREMIUM FOR
FLAWLESS CONDITION WITH TAG*

BEANIE HUNTER'S TIPS: A Bumble with his poem tag intact is extremely difficult to locate. In the unlikely event that this normally friendly bee stings his master, ask Mom for a "medicine kiss" and a cartoon character bandaid immediately.

CAW
(The Crow)

TOTAL MADE:	**250,000**	**Birthday: 1995**
(Est.) Survival 2007:	**25,000**	*Retired:* __1996__

ISSUE PRICE:	**$5.00**
1997 Value	**150.00**
(Est.) Year 2007	**850.00**

👍 **HIGHLY RECOMMENDED**   ✈ *ADD 50% TO 100% PREMIUM FOR FLAWLESS CONDITION WITH TAG*

BEANIE HUNTER'S TIPS: The poemless Caw was, unfortunately, retired for refusing to stop squawking about unfair treatment.   So here goes: "A crow is a pest / But Caw is the best / Wherever he's flown / May he perch on a throne."   Move over, Edgar Allen Poe!

☼ <u>CHILLY</u> ☼
(The Polar Bear)

TOTAL MADE:	50,000	Birthday: 1993
(Est.) Survival 2007:	5,000	*Retired:* <u>Dec., 1994</u>

ISSUE PRICE:	**$5.00**
1997 Value	**600.00**
(Est.) Year 2007	**2,500.00**

 HIGHLY
RECOMMENDED

✈ *ADD 50% TO 100% PREMIUM FOR*
FLAWLESS CONDITION WITH TAG

<u>**BEANIE HUNTER'S TIPS:**</u> Styled and posed differently than the Teddies, Chilly and Peking are the only two retired *reclining* bears. Even though this guy loves cold climates, never treat Chilly to an evening in the refrigerator. (It could be his last.) Very difficult to keep this bear's white coat immaculate. Few today are perfect.

☼ <u>CHOCOLATE</u> ☼
(The Moose)

TOTAL MADE:	4,000,000	Birthday: 4-27-93
(Est.) Survival 2007:	400,000	*Likely to be retired:* <u>1998</u>

ISSUE PRICE:	$5.00
1997 Value	5.00
(Est.) Year 2007	40.00

 RECOMMENDED ✈ *ADD 10% TO 20% PREMIUM FOR FLAWLESS CONDITION WITH TAG*

<u>BEANIE HUNTER'S TIPS:</u> Chocolate is one of the 9 original Beanie Babies and is among the favorites of almost every kid. In fact, he's as popular as Rocky the Squirrel's cartoon pal, Bullwinkle! NOTE: Since mid-1993, Moose sightings have out-numbered UFO sightings 2 to 1.

☼ CHOPS ☼
(The Lamb)

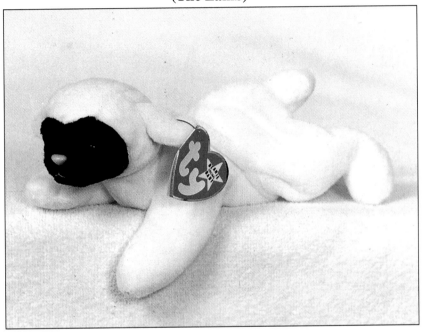

TOTAL MADE:	100,000	Birthday: 5-3-96
(Est.) Survival 2007:	10,000	*Retired:* <u>Dec., 1996</u>

ISSUE PRICE:	**$5.00**
1997 Value	**75.00**
(Est.) Year 2007	**750.00**

 **HIGHLY RECOMMENDED**

✈ *ADD 50% TO 100% PREMIUM FOR FLAWLESS CONDITION WITH TAG*

<u>**BEANIE HUNTER'S TIPS:**</u> Although Chops' gender is uncertain, the authors choose to identify this cute, black-faced wooly creature as "Fleece's boyfriend." Since the ratio of Fleece to Chops is 10 to 1 (Chops was only produced for 6 months), a shortage of males will cause matchmakers to drive prices higher over the years.

☼ CONGO ☼

(The Gorilla)

TOTAL MADE:	1,000,000	Birthday: 11-9-96
(Est.) Survival 2007:	100,000	*Likely to be retired:* **2000**

ISSUE PRICE:	**$5.00**
1997 Value	**5.00**
(Est.) Year 2007	**50.00**

 **HIGHLY
RECOMMENDED**

✈ *ADD 10% TO 20% PREMIUM FOR
FLAWLESS CONDITION WITH TAG*

BEANIE HUNTER'S TIPS: At first glance, Congo and Bongo appear to be fraternal twins (except for Congo's dark bi-color coat). Upon close examination, many subtle differences appear. Congo has a more pronounced brow, a button nose and is obviously far more dangerous. He may be available for a few years in a jungle near you.

☼ <u>CORAL</u> ☼
(The Tropical Fish)

TOTAL MADE:	250,000	Birthday: 3-2-95
(Est.) Survival 2007:	25,000	*Retired:* <u>*Dec., 1996*</u>

ISSUE PRICE:	**$5.00**
1997 Value	**50.00**
(Est.) Year 2007	**300.00**

 HIGHLY   ✈*ADD 50% TO 100% PREMIUM FOR*
RECOMMENDED   *FLAWLESS CONDITION WITH TAG*

<u>BEANIE HUNTER'S TIPS:</u> Coral was the first of the three fish to be retired. If his production is as low as we think, and demand gradually increases (fish are not currently "hot" Beanies), Coral's modest future value may soar above the waves. A "sleeper."

✹ <u>CRUNCH</u> ✹

(The Shark)

TOTAL MADE:	1,000,000	Birthday: 1-13-96
(Est.) Survival 2007:	100,000	*Likely to be retired:* <u>2000</u>

ISSUE PRICE:	$5.00
1997 Value	5.00
(Est.) Year 2007	40.00

 RECOMMENDED   ✈ *ADD 10% TO 20% PREMIUM FOR FLAWLESS CONDITION WITH TAG*

<u>BEANIE HUNTER'S TIPS:</u> Crunch the shark is a favorite of boy collectors. Just when you thought it was safe to go in the water, this menacing grey denizen of the deep has invaded your children's bath-tub. (Important: Even "aquatic" Beanie Babies are only "surface washable.")

☼ CUBBIE ☼
(The Brown Bear)

TOTAL MADE:	1,000,000	Birthday: 11-9-96
(Est.) Survival 2007:	100,000	*Likely to be retired:* __2000__

ISSUE PRICE:	$5.00
1997 Value	5.00
(Est.) Year 2007	50.00

 RECOMMENDED

✈ *ADD 10% TO 20% PREMIUM FOR*
FLAWLESS CONDITION WITH TAG

<u>BEANIE HUNTER'S TIPS:</u> Cubbie the Bear (first named Brownie) is one of the original 9 Beanie Babies designed in 1992. Although this cute guy may be going into hibernation shortly, there should be an ample supply for new collectors at reasonable prices.

☼ __CURLY__ ☼
(The Brown Bear)

TOTAL MADE:	1,000,000	Birthday: 4-12-96
(Est.) Survival 2007:	100,000	*Likely to be retired:* __1998__

ISSUE PRICE:	**$5.00**
1997 Value	**5.00**
(Est.) Year 2007	**40.00**

 **RECOMMENDED** ✈*ADD 10% TO 20% PREMIUM FOR FLAWLESS CONDITION WITH TAG*

__BEANIE HUNTER'S TIPS:__ Curly's fur is the less common nappy texture, rather than plush. His shelf life may be limited (probably because new blood adds constant excitement to the large and popular Teddy Bear line) and Curly may not be around in a year.

☼ **DAISY** ☼
(The Black & White Cow)

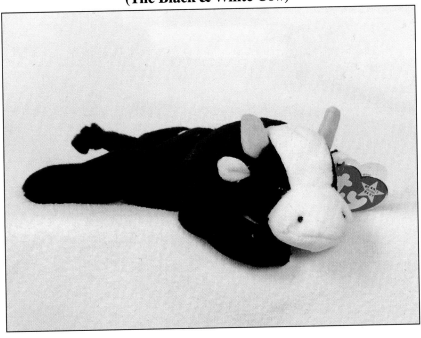

TOTAL MADE:	2,000,000	Birthday: 5-10-94
(Est.) Survival 2007:	200,000	*Likely to be retired:* __1998__

ISSUE PRICE:	**$5.00**
1997 Value	**5.00**
(Est.) Year 2007	**40.00**

 RECOMMENDED   ✈ *ADD 10% TO 20% PREMIUM FOR*
FLAWLESS CONDITION WITH TAG

__BEANIE HUNTER'S TIPS:__ Since Daisy has been grazing in Beanie Baby land a year longer than Bessie, she is likely to be put out to pasture first. Collect your pair of these milk smooth cuddlies while both are still mooing loudly.

☼ <u>DERBY</u> ☼
(The Horse)

TOTAL MADE:	3,000,000	Birthday: 9-6-95
(Est.) Survival 2007:	300,000	*Likely to be retired:* <u>**1998**</u>

ISSUE PRICE:	**$5.00**
1997 Value	**5.00**
(Est.) Year 2007	**40.00**

 **RECOMMENDED**   ✈ *ADD 10% TO 20% PREMIUM FOR*
FLAWLESS CONDITION WITH TAG

<u>**BEANIE HUNTER'S TIPS:**</u> In mid-1996, Derby's coat of fine yarn was changed to a coarser material. The original Derby is hard to find and is worth $50. Since Derby has been running hard for almost two years he is likely to be scratched from the Beanie race card soon. Watch for a dark horse named Star to make his debut.

☼ DIGGER ☼
(The Crab)

TOTAL MADE:	1,000,000	Birthday: 8-23-93
(Est.) Survival 2007:	100,000	*Likely to be retired:* **1997**

ISSUE PRICE:	**$5.00**
1997 Value	**5.00**
(Est.) Year 2007	**50.00**

 RECOMMENDED   ✈ *ADD 10% TO 20% PREMIUM FOR FLAWLESS CONDITION WITH TAG*

BEANIE HUNTER'S TIPS: The original (orange) Digger is worth $150. The new red crab seems to have been less mass produced than many other Beanies, and may prove to be a bargain at $5. Get your claws on one of these plush beachgoers before he's retired.

DOBY
(The Doberman)

TOTAL MADE:	1,000,000	Birthday: 10-9-96
(Est.) Survival 2007:	100,000	*Likely to be retired:* **2002**

ISSUE PRICE:	$5.00
1997 Value	5.00
(Est.) Year 2007	40.00

 RECOMMENDED

✈ *ADD 10% TO 20% PREMIUM FOR FLAWLESS CONDITION WITH TAG*

BEANIE HUNTER'S TIPS: One of the newest Beanie Baby puppies, Doby may be around for a while. (Or he may not.) Since lots of new breeds are slated for production, don't hesitate to acquire this prize Doberman for your personal protection.

EARS
(The Bunny)

| TOTAL MADE: | 2,000,000 | Birthday: 4-18-95 |
| (Est.) Survival 2007: | 200,000 | *Likely to be retired*: <u>**1998**</u> |

ISSUE PRICE:	**$5.00**
1997 Value	**5.00**
(Est.) Year 2007	**40.00**

👍 RECOMMENDED ✈ *ADD 10% TO 20% PREMIUM FOR*
FLAWLESS CONDITION WITH TAG

 **BEANIE HUNTER'S TIPS:** Unlike Hippity, Hoppity and Floppity, Ears is a lazy brown bunny who prefers the feel of cool earth against his warm belly. He needs extra attention now and then, and especially likes to be petted behind his long ears.

☼ **FLASH** ☼
(The Dolphin)

TOTAL MADE:	**3,000,000**	**Birthday: 5-13-93**
(Est.) Survival 2007:	**300,000**	*Likely to be retired:* <u>**1997**</u>

ISSUE PRICE:	**$5.00**
1997 Value	**5.00**
(Est.) Year 2007	**40.00**

 **RECOMMENDED**   ✈ *ADD 10% TO 20% PREMIUM FOR FLAWLESS CONDITION WITH TAG*

<u>**BEANIE HUNTER'S TIPS:**</u> Flash the Dolphin is one of the original 9 Beanie Babies. When training Flash to perform some of Flipper's famous tricks, be sure not to get him wet.

☼ FLEECE ☼
(The Lamb)

TOTAL MADE:	1,000,000	Birthday: 3-21-96
(Est.) Survival 2007:	100,000	*Likely to be retired:* **2000**

ISSUE PRICE:	$5.00
1997 Value	5.00
(Est.) Year 2007	40.00

 RECOMMENDED   ✈*ADD 10% TO 20% PREMIUM FOR*
FLAWLESS CONDITION WITH TAG

BEANIE HUNTER'S TIPS: This look-alike for Shari Lewis' sidekick, Lamb Chop, came on the scene when Chops was retired. He's been cloned by the Ty Company long before "Dolly" and is plush proof that scientific reproduction can benefit mankind. Like "Mary's" little lamb, Fleece may sneak into school in a backpack.

FLIP
(The White Cat)

TOTAL MADE: 1,000,000   Birthday: 2-28-95
(Est.) Survival 2007: 100,000   *Likely to be retired:* __1998__

ISSUE PRICE:	**$5.00**
1997 Value	**5.00**
(Est.) Year 2007	**75.00**

 HIGHLY   ✈ *ADD 25% TO 50% PREMIUM FOR*
RECOMMENDED   *FLAWLESS CONDITION WITH TAG*

__BEANIE HUNTER'S TIPS:__ Although Flip is not scheduled to be retired, he is still hard to find. Because of his white fur, find him a special spot in your room to protect his coat from soiling. (No litter box required.) And don't let him eat any hairballs!

☼ <u>FLOPPITY</u> ☼
(The Lilac Bunny)

TOTAL MADE:	2,000,000	Birthday: 5-28-96
(Est.) Survival 2007:	200,000	*Likely to be retired:* <u>**1999**</u>

ISSUE PRICE:	**$5.00**
1997 Value	**5.00**
(Est.) Year 2007	**40.00**

 RECOMMENDED

✈*ADD 10% TO 20% PREMIUM FOR*
FLAWLESS CONDITION WITH TAG

<u>**BEANIE HUNTER'S TIPS:**</u> This enchanting lilac bunny is difficult to find except during the holidays. Floppity enjoys romping with his two active playmates, Hippity and Hoppity. Just keep the frisky trio away from Mr. McGregor's garden!

☼ __FLUTTER__ ☼

(The Butterfly)

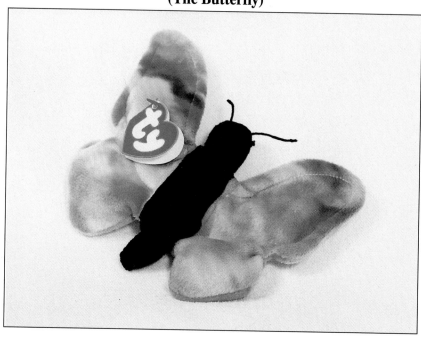

TOTAL MADE:	100,000	Birthday: 1995
(Est.) Survival 2007:	10,000	*Retired:* __1996__

ISSUE PRICE:	$5.00
1997 Value	300.00
(Est.) Year 2007	2,000.00

 **HIGHLY
RECOMMENDED**

✈ *ADD 50% TO 100% PREMIUM FOR
FLAWLESS CONDITION WITH TAG*

__BEANIE HUNTER'S TIPS:__ We're not sure why Flutter was retired so quickly, but apparently tie-dyed butterflies are not one of kids' favorites. This makes him all the more scarce and valuable. Net this one quickly for your butterfly and Beanie collection.

☼ <u>FRECKLES</u> ☼
(The Leopard)

TOTAL MADE:	1,000,000	Birthday: 6-3-96
(Est.) Survival 2007:	100,000	*Likely to be retired:* <u>**1998**</u>

ISSUE PRICE:	**$5.00**
1997 Value	**5.00**
(Est.) Year 2007	**50.00**

 RECOMMENDED   ✈*ADD 25% TO 50% PREMIUM FOR*
FLAWLESS CONDITION WITH TAG

<u>BEANIE HUNTER'S TIPS:</u> Adorable Freckles, loved by boys and girls, is a popular gift item and rarely has time to stalk the toy store shelves. A leopard never changes his spots, but one of these days Ty may decide to change its leopard! A collectible specimen of Freckles should have a perfectly positioned nose.

☼ GARCIA ☼
(The Tie-Dyed Teddy)

TOTAL MADE:	1,000,000	Birthday: 8-1-95
(Est.) Survival 2007:	100,000	*Likely to be retired:* __1997__

ISSUE PRICE:	**$5.00**
1997 Value	**25.00**
(Est.) Year 2007	**125.00**

 **HIGHLY
RECOMMENDED**

✈ *ADD 25% TO 50% PREMIUM FOR
FLAWLESS CONDITION WITH TAG*

__BEANIE HUNTER'S TIPS:__ Tremendously popular for his unusual colors, this folksy bear is tough to find at $5. Like snowflakes, no two Garcias are exactly the same! It is rumored that continued production might require a royalty to the Jerry Garcia family (like Ben & Jerry's ice cream flavor "Cherry Garcia.")

☼ GOLDIE ☼
(The Goldfish)

TOTAL MADE:	1,000,000	Birthday: 11-14-94
(Est.) Survival 2007:	100,000	*Likely to be retired:* __1997__

ISSUE PRICE:	**$5.00**
1997 Value	**5.00**
(Est.) Year 2007	**75.00**

 **HIGHLY RECOMMENDED**   ✈ *ADD 25% TO 50% PREMIUM FOR FLAWLESS CONDITION WITH TAG*

__BEANIE HUNTER'S TIPS:__ Goldie is crafted of the same plush orange fabric as the original Digger the Crab. Soon to be retired, Goldie can be hard to locate. A new fish is on the drawing board to replace this nautical delight. A desirable, under-rated Beanie.

☼ GRACIE ☼
(The Swan)

TOTAL MADE:	1,000,000	Birthday: 6-17-96
(Est.) Survival 2007:	100,000	*Likely to be retired:* __2000__

ISSUE PRICE:	$5.00
1997 Value	5.00
(Est.) Year 2007	40.00

 RECOMMENDED   ✈ *ADD 10% TO 20% PREMIUM FOR FLAWLESS CONDITION WITH TAG*

BEANIE HUNTER'S TIPS: When Kiwi was retired, Gracie floated across the Beanie pond. This simple, elegant swan is a modest design compared to the flamboyant toucan, but she is hardly an ugly duckling. Very easily soiled.

☼ <u>GRUNT</u> ☼

(The Razorback)

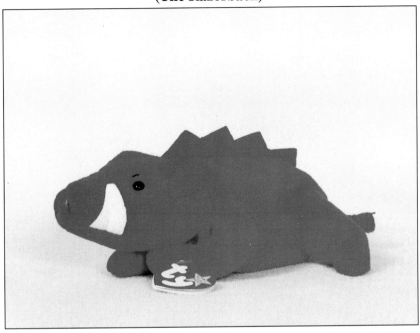

TOTAL MADE:	3,000,000	Birthday: 7-19-95
(Est.) Survival 2007:	300,000	*Likely to be retired:* <u>1999</u>

ISSUE PRICE:	**$5.00**
1997 Value	**5.00**
(Est.) Year 2007	**40.00**

 RECOMMENDED　　　✈*ADD 10% TO 20% PREMIUM FOR*
FLAWLESS CONDITION WITH TAG

<u>BEANIE HUNTER'S TIPS:</u> The bright red Grunt stands out in any crowd! Another popular boy toy, Grunt can easily disappear in tall grass or in the back of a closet. NOTE: If you see a real life razor-back in your own back yard, run inside, lock the door and call Animal Control!

☼ <u>HAPPY</u> ☼

(The Hippo)

TOTAL MADE:	2,000,000	Birthday: 2-25-94
(Est.) Survival 2007:	200,000	*Likely to be retired:* <u>1998</u>

ISSUE PRICE:	$5.00
1997 Value	5.00
(Est.) Year 2007	40.00

 RECOMMENDED   ✈*ADD 10% TO 20% PREMIUM FOR FLAWLESS CONDITION WITH TAG*

<u>BEANIE HUNTER'S TIPS:</u> Redesigned in lavendar, the original gray Happy the Hippo was retired in mid-1995. With a maximum of 50,000 examples of the scarcer version (5,000 within 10 years), the more precious Happy is highly recommended at $200.

☼ HIPPITY ☼
(The Mint Bunny)

TOTAL MADE:	**1,000,000**	**Birthday: 6-1-96**
(Est.) Survival 2007:	**100,000**	*Likely to be retired:* **1998**

ISSUE PRICE:	**$5.00**
1997 Value	**5.00**
(Est.) Year 2007	**75.00**

 **HIGHLY RECOMMENDED**

✈ *ADD 25% TO 50% PREMIUM FOR FLAWLESS CONDITION WITH TAG*

BEANIE HUNTER'S TIPS: This delicious, mint-colored bunny is not yet retired but is usually one hard wabbit to corner! He's currently the rarest of the four bunnies, but his production figure will increase.

☼ HOOT ☼
(The Owl)

TOTAL MADE:	2,000,000	Birthday: 8-9-95
(Est.) Survival 2007:	200,000	*Likely to be retired:* __1998__

ISSUE PRICE:	**$5.00**
1997 Value	**5.00**
(Est.) Year 2007	**40.00**

 RECOMMENDED   ✈ *ADD 10% TO 20% PREMIUM FOR FLAWLESS CONDITION WITH TAG*

__BEANIE HUNTER'S TIPS:__ At only 6" tall, Hoot is one of the smaller Beanies. (Slither is the largest, in terms of length.) This petite owl wonders why he hasn't been invited to sing with the band on Sesame Street. Serious collectors think this guy's a real hoot!

☼ HOPPITY ☼

(The Rose Bunny)

TOTAL MADE:	2,000,000	Birthday: 4-3-96
(Est.) Survival 2007:	200,000	*Likely to be retired:* **1999**

ISSUE PRICE:	**$5.00**
1997 Value	**5.00**
(Est.) Year 2007	**40.00**

 RECOMMENDED   ✈ *ADD 10% TO 20% PREMIUM FOR FLAWLESS CONDITION WITH TAG*

BEANIE HUNTER'S TIPS: A rose-colored bunny with lots of personality, adding Hoppity to your Beanie collection will multiply your fun! Like all rabbits, this one enjoys a crispy carrot for a snack. Plush veggies only!

☼ HUMPHREY ☼

(The Camel)

TOTAL MADE:	25,000	Birthday: June, 1994
(Est.) Survival 2007:	2,500	*Retired:* <u>Dec., 1995</u>

ISSUE PRICE:	$5.00
1997 Value	650.00
(Est.) Year 2007	3,500.00

 HIGHLY
RECOMMENDED

✈ *ADD 50% TO 100% PREMIUM FOR*
FLAWLESS CONDITION WITH TAG

<u>BEANIE HUNTER'S TIPS:</u> One of the rarest and most sought after Beanies, Humphrey's extra long legs and bumpy hump are simply captivating! Someday this plush tan dromedary may become the "Superstar" of the Beanie Baby Kingdom! Not so easy to acquire one in flawless condition with original tags.

INCH
(The Inchworm)

TOTAL MADE:	3,000,000	Birthday: 9-3-95
(Est.) Survival 2007:	300,000	*Likely to be retired:* **1999**

ISSUE PRICE:	**$5.00**
1997 Value	**5.00**
(Est.) Year 2007	**40.00**

 **RECOMMENDED**   ✈*ADD 10% TO 20% PREMIUM FOR FLAWLESS CONDITION WITH TAG*

BEANIE HUNTER'S TIPS: Inch was introduced with thick, black felt antennae. In mid-1996, this was changed to black yarn. The original Inch is worth $100. Few kids can "foot" the bill for this scarce version, but the new, delightful specimen will set you back a mere five-spot!

INKY
(The Octopus)

TOTAL MADE:	3,000,000	Birthday: 11-29-94
(Est.) Survival 2007:	300,000	*Likely to be retired:* <u>**1999**</u>

ISSUE PRICE:	**$5.00**
1997 Value	**5.00**
(Est.) Year 2007	**40.00**

 RECOMMENDED   *ADD 10% TO 20% PREMIUM FOR FLAWLESS CONDITION WITH TAG*

<u>**BEANIE HUNTER'S TIPS:**</u> First produced in a unique shade of tan, in mid-1995 Inky's fabric was changed to Squealer-the-Pig-Pink. (The tan Octopus is worth $200.) Inky is a bit too commercially goofy for the authors' taste but some kids can't keep their tentacles off him.

KIWI
(The Toucan)

TOTAL MADE:	500,000	Birthday: 9-16-95
(Est.) Survival 2007:	50,000	*Retired:* Dec., 1996

ISSUE PRICE:	$5.00
1997 Value	50.00
(Est.) Year 2007	500.00

 **HIGHLY RECOMMENDED**   ✈ *ADD 50% TO 100% PREMIUM FOR FLAWLESS CONDITION WITH TAG*

BEANIE HUNTER'S TIPS: Kiwi and Caw the Crow share the same bird body form, except Kiwi has a slightly larger bill. This Toucan's amazing rainbow colors make him an outstanding candidate for price appreciation. One of our very favorite Beanies, Kiwi looks great perched on your shoulder.

☼ LEFTY ☼

(The Democratic Donkey)

TOTAL MADE:	250,000	Birthday: July 4, 1996
(Est.) Survival 2007:	25,000	*Retired:* <u>Dec., 1996</u>

ISSUE PRICE:	**$5.00**
1997 Value	**50.00**
(Est.) Year 2007	**750.00**

 **HIGHLY RECOMMENDED**

✈ *ADD 50% TO 100% PREMIUM FOR FLAWLESS CONDITION WITH TAG*

<u>BEANIE HUNTER'S TIPS:</u> Like his Republican counterpart ("Righty"), the patriotic Lefty was introduced to America during the 1996 Presidential campaign. Both pieces had a limited run and will undoubtedly become highly collectible. Look for a re-issue in the year 2000. Bill Clinton's favorite Beanie!

LEGS
(The Frog)

TOTAL MADE:	4,000,000	Birthday: 4-25-93
(Est.) Survival 2007:	400,000	*Likely to be retired:* <u>**1997**</u>

ISSUE PRICE:	**$5.00**
1997 Value	**5.00**
(Est.) Year 2007	**40.00**

 **RECOMMENDED** ✈*ADD 10% TO 20% PREMIUM FOR FLAWLESS CONDITION WITH TAG*

<u>**BEANIE HUNTER'S TIPS:**</u> Legs is one of the original 9 Beanie Babies and has been a staple of the collection. However, we think he's about to disappear beneath his water lily pads. Bonus: It has been reported that a single kiss could turn legs into a handsome prince!

✪ <u>LIBEARTY</u> ✪

(The U.S.A. Bear)

TOTAL MADE:	**500,000**	**Birthday: August, 1996**	
(Est.) Survival 2007:	**50,000**	*Retired*: <u>Dec., 1996</u>	

ISSUE PRICE:	**$5.00**
1997 Value	**35.00**
(Est.) Year 2007	**400.00**

 **HIGHLY
RECOMMENDED**

✈ *ADD 50% TO 100% PREMIUM FOR
FLAWLESS CONDITION WITH TAG*

<u>**BEANIE HUNTER'S TIPS:**</u> Libearty was the first Beanie to debut with a poem tag, but has no exact birthday. He's one of three Beanies bearing an American flag patch. (Note: "Maple" is the exclusive Canadian version of Libearty.) Libearty is fond of being held to your heart when you recite the pledge of allegiance, but no ketchup fingers!

LIZZY
(The Lizard)

TOTAL MADE:	2,000,000	**Birthday: 5-11-95**
(Est.) Survival 2007:	200,000	*Likely to be retired:* <u>**1999**</u>

ISSUE PRICE:	**$5.00**
1997 Value	**5.00**
(Est.) Year 2007	**40.00**

👍 RECOMMENDED

✈ *ADD 10% TO 20% PREMIUM FOR FLAWLESS CONDITION WITH TAG*

BEANIE HUNTER'S TIPS: The short-lived tie-dyed Lizzy is scarce. Perhaps 50,000 of the original version were produced (current value $300) and is highly recommended. When the new, bright blue Lizzy (with yellow belly and black spots) arrived in early 1996, only Coral (now retired) and Garcia were left to uphold the tie-dye tradition.

☼ LUCKY ☼
(The Ladybug)

TOTAL MADE:	3,000,000	Birthday: 5-1-93
(Est.) Survival 2007:	300,000	*Likely to be retired:* **1998**

ISSUE PRICE:	**$5.00**
1997 Value	**5.00**
(Est.) Year 2007	**40.00**

👍 RECOMMENDED   ✈ *ADD 10% TO 20% PREMIUM FOR FLAWLESS CONDITION WITH TAG*

BEANIE HUNTER'S TIPS: Lucky alighted in late 1994 with seven black felt spots glued to her back. These spots easily came unglued, so in the Summer of 1996 Lucky's spots became part of the fabric design. There were three minor style changes in 1996. Today, the original Lucky with glued spots is worth $100.

☼ **MAGIC** ☼
(The Dragon)

TOTAL MADE:	1,000,000	Birthday: 9-5-95
(Est.) Survival 2007:	100,000	*Likely to be Retired:* __1997__

ISSUE PRICE:	**$5.00**
1997 Value	**25.00**
(Est.) Year 2007	**75.00**

 **HIGHLY RECOMMENDED**

✈️ *ADD 25% TO 50% PREMIUM FOR FLAWLESS CONDITION WITH TAG*

__BEANIE HUNTER'S TIPS:__ Named after "Puff," the dragon made famous by Peter, Paul and Mary, Magic only lives by the sea when he visits his weekend house in the Hamptons. He prefers to frolic in the land of Hana-Li, but will accept your pillow as a substitute. Boys favor magic. White with iridescent wings, handle with care!

☼ <u>MANNY</u> ☼
(The Manatee)

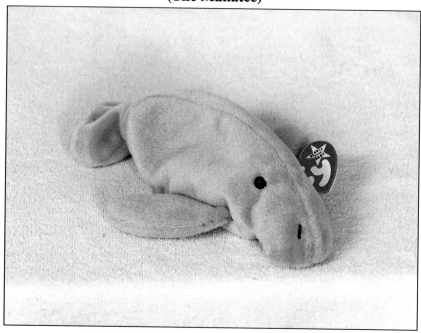

TOTAL MADE:	1,000,000	Birthday: 6-8-95
(Est.) Survival 2007:	100,000	*Likely to be retired:* <u>1997</u>

ISSUE PRICE:	$5.00
1997 Value	5.00
(Est.) Year 2007	75.00

 **HIGHLY RECOMMENDED**

✈ *ADD 25% TO 50% PREMIUM FOR FLAWLESS CONDITION WITH TAG*

<u>**BEANIE HUNTER'S TIPS:**</u> Florida's #1 endangered species, songwriter Jimmy Buffet has supported the "Save The Manatees" cause for many years. A limited edition Manny could be tied to a fund-raising effort. In tropical waters, manatees (sea cows) are gentle, shy creatures. No collection is complete without one.

MEL

(The Koala)

TOTAL MADE:	1,000,000	Birthday: 1-15-96
(Est.) Survival 2007:	100,000	*Likely to be retired:* **2000**

ISSUE PRICE:	$5.00
1997 Value	5.00
(Est.) Year 2007	40.00

 RECOMMENDED

✈ *ADD 10% TO 20% PREMIUM FOR FLAWLESS CONDITION WITH TAG*

BEANIE HUNTER'S TIPS: With his goofy smirk, Mel is not only the cheeriest bear in the collection, he's the only one with a real mouth! We'd be surprised to see him retire before the millenium, but you never know.

☼ <u>MYSTIC</u> ☼

(The Unicorn)

| TOTAL MADE: | 4,000,000 | Birthday: 5-21-94 |
| (Est.) Survival 2007: | 400,000 | *Likely to be retired:* <u>**1998**</u> |

ISSUE PRICE:	**$5.00**
1997 Value	**5.00**
(Est.) Year 2007	**40.00**

 **RECOMMENDED**   ✈*ADD 10% TO 20% PREMIUM FOR*
FLAWLESS CONDITION WITH TAG

<u>BEANIE HUNTER'S TIPS:</u> Another popular milk-white Beanie creature which will become increasingly difficult to find in spanking new condition. Mystic is surprisingly elusive with such a high production. As in reality, the Unicorn may be rarer than we think.

NIP

(The Gold Cat)

TOTAL MADE:	3,000,000	Birthday: 3-6-94
(Est.) Survival 2007:	300,000	*Likely to be retired:* __1997__

ISSUE PRICE:	$5.00
1997 Value	5.00
(Est.) Year 2007	40.00

 RECOMMENDED
(*See also: ZIP)

✈ *ADD 10% TO 20% PREMIUM FOR*
FLAWLESS CONDITION WITH TAG

__BEANIE HUNTER'S TIPS:__ The current ($5) Nip is smaller than the original version, now worth $200 and highly recommended. The first of three Nips had a white mug and a white belly. An interim gold-pawed Nip had a very limited run (10,000 or less) and is worth $750. We prefer the larger Nip (50,000 made), as few perfect ones exist.

☼ **NUTS** ☼
(The Squirrel)

TOTAL MADE:	1,000,000	Birthday: 1-21-96
(Est.) Survival 2007:	100,000	*Likely to be retired:* **2000**

ISSUE PRICE:	**$5.00**
1997 Value	**5.00**
(Est.) Year 2007	**40.00**

 **RECOMMENDED**   ✈ *ADD 10% TO 20% PREMIUM FOR FLAWLESS CONDITION WITH TAG*

BEANIE HUNTER'S TIPS: "Nuts the squirrel... is eight inches of trouble!" This issue has won the hearts of America's Beanie collecting youth. His fluffy tail sets him apart, and captures the spirit of the neighborhood acorn lover. It's okay to go nuts and buy a few extra to dig up in Spring, 2007. (Will Nuts be replaced by a chipmunk?)

☼ **PATTI** ☼
(The Platypus)

TOTAL MADE:	4,000,000	Birthday: 1-6-93
(Est.) Survival 2007:	400,000	*Likely to be retired:* **1998**

ISSUE PRICE:	**$5.00**
1997 Value	**5.00**
(Est.) Year 2007	**40.00**

 RECOMMENDED   ✈*ADD 10% TO 20% PREMIUM FOR FLAWLESS CONDITION WITH TAG*

BEANIE HUNTER'S TIPS: Originally introduced with more of a reddish tint, Patti now has a distinctively purple hue. (An example in the scarce color is worth $500.) Patti the Platypus is one of the original 9 Beanie Babies. Patti nips when incorrectly referred to as a "duck."

☼ **PEANUT** ☼

(The Elephant)

TOTAL MADE:	2,000,000	Birthday: 1-25-96
(Est.) Survival 2007:	200,000	*Likely to be retired:* <u>**2001**</u>

ISSUE PRICE:	**$5.00**
1997 Value	**5.00**
(Est.) Year 2007	**40.00**

 RECOMMENDED   ✈ *ADD 10% TO 20% PREMIUM FOR FLAWLESS CONDITION WITH TAG*

<u>**BEANIE HUNTER'S TIPS:**</u> Peanut the Dark Blue Elephant, considered by many to be the prize Beanie Baby, was distributed for only one month, June, 1995. We estimate that only 2,000 of the original were made (current mint condition value $1,500) and highly recommend it to serious collectors. It could be worth $5,000+.

☼ PEKING ☼

(The Panda)

TOTAL MADE:	50,000	Birthday: 1994
(Est.) Survival 2007:	5,000	*Retired:* <u>1994</u>

ISSUE PRICE:	**$5.00**
1997 Value	**600.00**
(Est.) Year 2007	**3,000.00**

 HIGHLY
RECOMMENDED

✈ *ADD 50% TO 100% PREMIUM FOR*
FLAWLESS CONDITION WITH TAG

BEANIE HUNTER'S TIPS: Peking and Chilly are the two early, rare "reclining" bears. (Peking is cuter.) Highly desirable, as most are dirty or frayed. Should your family visit the National Zoo in Washington, D.C., Peking would surely relish a peek at his two relatives, Ling Ling and Hsing Hsing.

☼ <u>PINCHERS</u> ☼

(The Lobster)

TOTAL MADE:	4,000,000	Birthday: 6-19-93
(Est.) Survival 2007:	400,000	*Likely to be retired:* <u>1998</u>

ISSUE PRICE:	$5.00
1997 Value	5.00
(Est.) Year 2007	40.00

 RECOMMENDED   ✈*ADD 10% TO 20% PREMIUM FOR FLAWLESS CONDITION WITH TAG*

<u>BEANIE HUNTER'S TIPS:</u> Pinchers the Lobster is one of the original 9 Beanie Babies. Caution: If you take Pinchers to the beach to catch some rays, be sure to leave before your sunburn matches his.

☼ __PINKY__ ☼

(The Flamingo)

TOTAL MADE:	3,000,000	Birthday: 2-13-95
(Est.) Survival 2007:	300,000	*Likely to be retired:* __1998__

ISSUE PRICE:	$5.00
1997 Value	5.00
(Est.) Year 2007	60.00

 RECOMMENDED ✈*ADD 25% TO 50% PREMIUM FOR FLAWLESS CONDITION WITH TAG*

__BEANIE HUNTER'S TIPS:__ While the long-stemmed Pinky is among the highest production Beanies, once she's retired collectors will find that harshly handled examples are the rule. Treat your Pinky with special care and jet her off on a Miami Vacation if she says she misses her family.

☼ POUCH ☼

(The Kangaroo)

TOTAL MADE:	1,000,000	Birthday: 11-6-95
(Est.) Survival 2007:	100,000	*Likely to be retired:* **2001**

ISSUE PRICE:	**$5.00**
1997 Value	**5.00**
(Est.) Year 2007	**40.00**

 **RECOMMENDED**   ✈ *ADD 10% TO 20% PREMIUM FOR FLAWLESS CONDITION WITH TAG*

BEANIE HUNTER'S TIPS: Pouch is the only Beanie featuring two animals in one. This loving marsupial Mommie (or is Pouch the baby?) and her precious cargo will be with us for a few years. The little one is so cute you really have no choice but to hop on down to your local toy store for a pair of the pair.

–84–

☼ QUACKERS ☼
(The Duck)

TOTAL MADE:	4,000,000	Birthday: 4-19-93
(Est.) Survival 2007:	400,000	*Likely to be retired:* __2003__

ISSUE PRICE:	**$5.00**
1997 Value	**5.00**
(Est.) Year 2007	**40.00**

 **RECOMMENDED**   ✈*ADD 10% TO 20% PREMIUM FOR*
FLAWLESS CONDITION WITH TAG

__BEANIE HUNTER'S TIPS:__ Quackers was first designed and manufactured without wings. Only 780 wingless examples were produced, choice ones worth $1,000. If Beanie collecting grows more sophisticated, expect the original to hit $5,000. Should the popular $5 water fowl stick it out for a decade, that's just ducky with us!

–85 –

☼ **<u>RADAR</u>** ☼

(The Bat)

TOTAL MADE:	500,000	Birthday: 10-30-95
(Est.) Survival 2007:	50,000	*Likely to be retired:* <u>*1997*</u>

ISSUE PRICE:	**$5.00**
1997 Value	**25.00**
(Est.) Year 2007	**200.00**

 **HIGHLY**
RECOMMENDED

✈ *ADD 25% TO 50% PREMIUM FOR*
FLAWLESS CONDITION WITH TAG

<u>**BEANIE HUNTER'S TIPS:**</u> Along with Spooky, this sinister night dweller was created expressly for Halloween. Radar is no count Dracula, but you could be bloody well disappointed if you don't acquire him at current prices.

REX
(The Tyrannosaurus)

TOTAL MADE:	100,000	Birthday: 1995
(Est.) Survival 2007:	10,000	*Retired:* __1996__

ISSUE PRICE:	**$5.00**
1997 Value	**200.00**
(Est.) Year 2007	**1,000.00**

 **HIGHLY RECOMMENDED**

✈ *ADD 10% TO 20% PREMIUM FOR FLAWLESS CONDITION WITH TAG*

__BEANIE HUNTER'S TIPS:__ Like Steg, Rex is a multi-colored dinosaur. (Bronty's fabric is shades of blue.) Jurassic Park buffs have spread the word to keep lawyers away from Rex! Hugely popular, and rarely "discovered" at $5 in some secret bin.

RIGHTY

(The Republican Elephant)

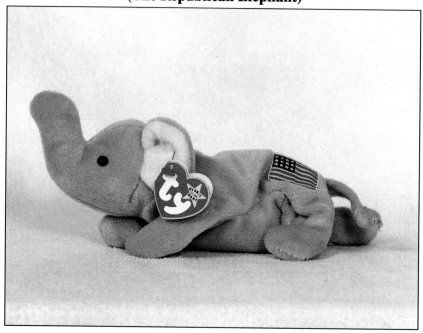

| TOTAL MADE: | 250,000 | Birthday: July 4, 1996 |
| (Est.) Survival 2007: | 25,000 | *Retired*: Dec., 1996 |

ISSUE PRICE:	$5.00
1997 Value	50.00
(Est.) Year 2007	750.00

 **HIGHLY RECOMMENDED**   ✈ *ADD 50% TO 100% PREMIUM FOR FLAWLESS CONDITION WITH TAG*

BEANIE HUNTER'S TIPS: Righty and Lefty have been credited with triggering off the accelerated interest in Beanie Baby collectibles. Both are relatively scarce and will be among the prize examples of advanced collections. (We know kids who have detached the flags!) Righty is banned from the White House until the year 2004.

☼ RINGO ☼
(The Raccoon)

TOTAL MADE:	2,000,000	Birthday: 7-14-95
(Est.) Survival 2007:	200,000	*Likely to be retired:* __2000__

ISSUE PRICE:	$5.00
1997 Value	5.00
(Est.) Year 2007	40.00

 RECOMMENDED   ✈*ADD 10% TO 20% PREMIUM FOR FLAWLESS CONDITION WITH TAG*

BEANIE HUNTER'S TIPS: Middle-aged Beanie collectors ("Hel-lo!"), and retro teens, are automatically reminded of Ringo Starr, the Beatles' second drummer. Like his namesake, this raccoon cannot carry a tune! Also, Ringo's face mask needs to be expanded. Very popular.

☼ <u>ROVER</u> ☼
(The Red Dog)

TOTAL MADE:	1,000,000	Birthday: 5-30-96
(Est.) Survival 2007:	100,000	*Likely to be retired:* <u>*1998*</u>

ISSUE PRICE:	$5.00
1997 Value	5.00
(Est.) Year 2007	50.00

 RECOMMENDED   ✈*ADD 10% TO 20% PREMIUM FOR FLAWLESS CONDITION WITH TAG*

<u>**BEANIE HUNTER'S TIPS:**</u> Since many new breeds will be added to the Beanie Baby dog contingency, we foresee Rover being retired from the show ring only two years after he was housebroken. Leash one or two today!

☼ **SCOOP** ☼
(The Pelican)

TOTAL MADE:	1,000,000	Birthday: 7-1-96
(Est.) Survival 2007:	100,000	*Likely to be retired:* **1998**

ISSUE PRICE:	**$5.00**
1997 Value	**5.00**
(Est.) Year 2007	**50.00**

 RECOMMENDED   ✈*ADD 10% TO 20% PREMIUM FOR FLAWLESS CONDITION WITH TAG*

BEANIE HUNTER'S TIPS: We've got the scoop on the world's most popular pelican. His whimsical bill just happens to be filled to the brim with plush sardines! We suggest you keep an air freshener near his nest.

☼ **SCOTTIE** ☼
(The Black Terrier)

TOTAL MADE:	1,000,000	Birthday: 6-15-96
(Est.) Survival 2007:	100,000	*Likely to be retired:* <u>**2002**</u>

ISSUE PRICE:	**$5.00**
1997 Value	**5.00**
(Est.) Year 2007	**40.00**

 RECOMMENDED   ✈ *ADD 10% TO 20% PREMIUM FOR*
FLAWLESS CONDITION WITH TAG

BEANIE HUNTER'S TIPS: Scottie has the same nappy fur as Curly the Teddy. While demure in stature, this all-black He-Man is known for his loud bark and commensurate bite. Warning: Even if Scottie growls, and shows his sharp teeth, don't pour any Black & White Scotch into his mini water bowl.

☼ <u>SEAMORE</u> ☼
(The Seal)

TOTAL MADE:	1,000,000	Birthday: 12-14-96
(Est.) Survival 2007:	100,000	*Likely to be retired:* <u>*1999*</u>

ISSUE PRICE:	**$5.00**
1997 Value	**5.00**
(Est.) Year 2007	**50.00**

 **RECOMMENDED**   ✈*ADD 10% TO 20% PREMIUM FOR FLAWLESS CONDITION WITH TAG*

<u>**BEANIE HUNTER'S TIPS:**</u> Collectors flaps their flippers wildly for this plush seal. If he retires, we'd like to "see more" Seamore, perhaps re-designed in an interesting new color combo, like brown and tan. A perfect specimen will become scarce, because white soils.

☼ <u>SEAWEED</u> ☼

(The Otter)

TOTAL MADE:	1,000,000	Birthday: 3-19-96
(Est.) Survival 2007:	100,000	*Likely to be retired:* <u>2002</u>

ISSUE PRICE:	**$5.00**
1997 Value	**5.00**
(Est.) Year 2007	**50.00**

 RECOMMENDED   ✈ *ADD 10% TO 20% PREMIUM FOR FLAWLESS CONDITION WITH TAG*

<u>BEANIE HUNTER'S TIPS:</u> Seaweed is the only upside-down Beanie Baby, and a clever design he is! An utterly pleasing baby otter, even if he doesn't actually float like Ivory Soap. A collectible example should have a perfectly positioned nose.

☼ <u>SLITHER</u> ☼
(The Snake)

TOTAL MADE:	100,000	Birthday: June, 1994
(Est.) Survival 2007:	10,000	*Retired:* <u>Dec., 1995</u>

ISSUE PRICE:	**$5.00**
1997 Value	**500.00**
(Est.) Year 2007	**2,500.00**

 **HIGHLY RECOMMENDED**   ✈ *ADD 50% TO 100% PREMIUM FOR FLAWLESS CONDITION WITH TAG*

<u>**BEANIE HUNTER'S TIPS:**</u> At 23" long, Slither is the largest Beanie from end to end. He shares the same fabric pattern as Ally and Speedy (except Slither is darker), and his yellow belly matches Quackers. Even if another snake slithers onto the scene, the rarity of the original will not be usurped. A snake worth stretching for.

SLY

(The Fox)

TOTAL MADE:	1,000,000	Birthday: 9-12-96
(Est.) Survival 2007:	100,000	*Likely to be retired:* **2001**

ISSUE PRICE:	**$5.00**
1997 Value	**5.00**
(Est.) Year 2007	**40.00**

 RECOMMENDED   ✈ *ADD 10% TO 20% PREMIUM FOR FLAWLESS CONDITION WITH TAG*

BEANIE HUNTER'S TIPS: Originally introduced with a brown belly, the now anatomically correct Sly has been re-outfitted with a white one. A Brown Belly Sly is worth $100. A Foxy snare!

SNIP

(The Siamese Cat)

TOTAL MADE:	1,000,000	Birthday: 10-22-96
(Est.) Survival 2007:	100,000	*Likely to be retired:* **2002**

ISSUE PRICE:	**$5.00**
1997 Value	**5.00**
(Est.) Year 2007	**40.00**

 RECOMMENDED

✈ *ADD 10% TO 20% PREMIUM FOR*
FLAWLESS CONDITION WITH TAG

BEANIE HUNTER'S TIPS: Snip is the newest Beanie Baby cat. Of the four felines in the Ty line, only Snip has a spot on her forehead, and a dark nose. Unlike Nip and Zip, there is no matching paw, body or other variety (yet.) We predict the next cat will be a Calico.

☼ **SNORT** ☼

(The Bull)

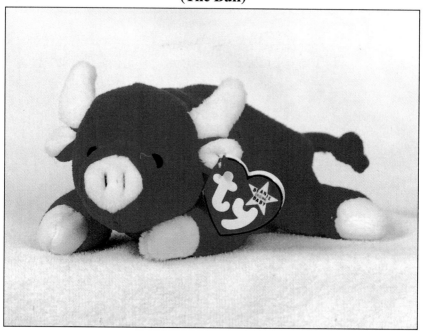

TOTAL MADE:	1,000,000	Birthday: 5-15-95
(Est.) Survival 2007:	100,000	*Likely to be retired:* **2002**

ISSUE PRICE:	$5.00
1997 Value	5.00
(Est.) Year 2007	40.00

 RECOMMENDED   ✈*ADD 10% TO 20% PREMIUM FOR FLAWLESS CONDITION WITH TAG*

BEANIE HUNTER'S TIPS: Snort, Tabasco's replacement, is identical to his predecessor except for his cream-trimmed feet. Due to overwhelming demand for the retired version, Snort is a high-production animal with a lot of personality. Although issued in January, 1997, Snort was assigned Tabasco's 1995 birthday.

☼ SPARKY ☼
(The Dalmatian)

TOTAL MADE:	1,000,000	Birthday: 2-27-96
(Est.) Survival 2007:	100,000	*Likely to be retired:* **2001**

ISSUE PRICE:	**$5.00**
1997 Value	**5.00**
(Est.) Year 2007	**50.00**

 RECOMMENDED   ✈*ADD 10% TO 20% PREMIUM FOR FLAWLESS CONDITION WITH TAG*

BEANIE HUNTER'S TIPS: It is rumored that the fairly recently released Sparky's days may be numbered . . . as in "101!" If he suddenly leaves us in 1997 or 1998, watch for a slew of other dalmatians to fill the interest in a breed regularly promoted by Disney.

☼ **SPEEDY** ☼
(The Turtle)

TOTAL MADE:	3,000,000	**Birthday: 8-14-94**
(Est.) Survival 2007:	300,000	*Likely to be retired:* **1997**

ISSUE PRICE:	**$5.00**
1997 Value	**5.00**
(Est.) Year 2007	**40.00**

 RECOMMENDED   ✈*ADD 10% TO 20% PREMIUM FOR FLAWLESS CONDITION WITH TAG*

BEANIE HUNTER'S TIPS: If Speedy is retired in 1997 (as many believe), he is definitely entitled to a proper farewell party. Of course, don't expect him to show up on time, like Hippity, Hoppity, etc. Slow and steady is only guaranteed to win friends.

☼ SPIKE ☼

(The Rhinoceros)

TOTAL MADE:	1,000,000	Birthday: 8-13-96
(Est.) Survival 2007:	100,000	*Likely to be retired:* **2000**

ISSUE PRICE:	**$5.00**
1997 Value	**5.00**
(Est.) Year 2007	**40.00**

 RECOMMENDED   ✈ *ADD 10% TO 20% PREMIUM FOR FLAWLESS CONDITION WITH TAG*

BEANIE HUNTER'S TIPS: A recent and welcome addition to the African jungle beast category, make way for Spike! Rugged and maculine beyond his years (months), this playful rhino fears nothing and enjoys roughhousing with vigorous youngsters. Whatever you dish out, Spike can take it!

☼ **SPLASH** ☼
(The Orca Whale)

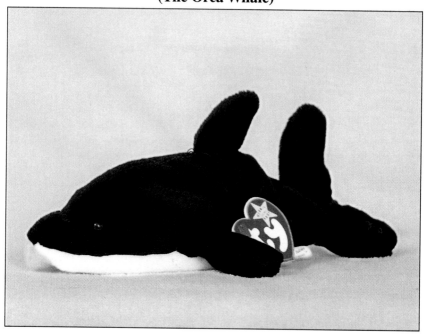

TOTAL MADE:	4,000,000	Birthday: 7-8-93
(Est.) Survival 2007:	400,000	*Likely to be retired:* **1998**

ISSUE PRICE:	**$5.00**
1997 Value	**5.00**
(Est.) Year 2007	**40.00**

 RECOMMENDED   ✈ *ADD 10% TO 20% PREMIUM FOR*
FLAWLESS CONDITION WITH TAG

BEANIE HUNTER'S TIPS: Splash is one of the original 9 Beanie Babies issued in 1993. He's got a high IQ, too, so don't let him watch "Free Willy" (or listen to Michael Jackson's theme song) as this free-spirited marauder might venture an escape to the open sea!

☼ <u>SPOOKY</u> ☼
(The Ghost)

TOTAL MADE:	1,000,000	Birthday: 10-31-95
(Est.) Survival 2007:	100,000	*Likely to be retired:* <u>**1997**</u>

ISSUE PRICE:	**$5.00**
1997 Value	**50.00**
(Est.) Year 2007	**150.00**

 **RECOMMENDED**   ✈ *ADD 10% TO 20% PREMIUM FOR FLAWLESS CONDITION WITH TAG*

<u>**BEANIE HUNTER'S TIPS:**</u> First produced as "Spook" (in error), this is the only non-animal Beanie. Designed by Jenna Boldebuck, whose name appears on the Ty tag (Jenna lives in the same house as Ty Warner, see photo in this book), Spooky was conceived for Halloween. A strange variety of mouths makes this guy fascinating.

☼ **SPOT** ☼
(The Dog)

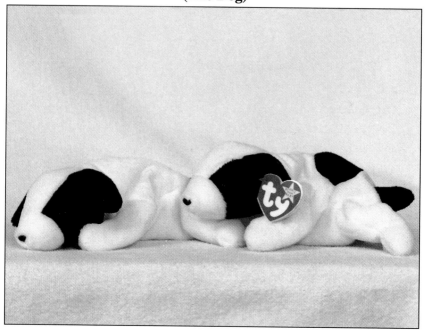

TOTAL MADE:	4,000,000	Birthday: 1-3-93
(Est.) Survival 2007:	400,000	*Likely to be retired:* **1998**

ISSUE PRICE:	**$5.00**
1997 Value	**5.00**
(Est.) Year 2007	**40.00**

 RECOMMENDED   ✈ *ADD 10% TO 20% PREMIUM FOR FLAWLESS CONDITION WITH TAG*

BEANIE HUNTER'S TIPS: As originally created (without a black spot, estimated run 5,000 pieces), Spot is one of the rarest issues. A "spotless" Spot is worth $1,200. Spot is also one of the 9 original Beanie Babies and has the earliest birthday. Highly recommended in superb condition without the spot.

☼ **SQUEALER** ☼

(The Pig)

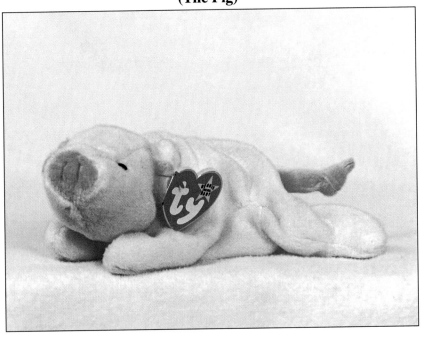

TOTAL MADE:	4,000,000	Birthday: 4-23-93
(Est.) Survival 2007:	400,000	*Likely to be retired:* __2003__

ISSUE PRICE:	**$5.00**
1997 Value	**5.00**
(Est.) Year 2007	**40.00**

 RECOMMENDED

✈ *ADD 10% TO 20% PREMIUM FOR*
FLAWLESS CONDITION WITH TAG

BEANIE HUNTER'S TIPS: Squealer the Pig is one of the 9 original Beanie Babies. Warning: Do not overfeed Squealer. Too many Sloppy Joe's will ruin his sleek physique and transform him into Porky the Pig.

STEG

(The Stegosaurus)

TOTAL MADE:	**100,000**	**Birthday: 1995**
(Est.) Survival 2007:	**10,000**	*Retired:* **Dec., 1996**

ISSUE PRICE:	**$5.00**
1997 Value	**200.00**
(Est.) Year 2007	**1,000.00**

 **HIGHLY RECOMMENDED**

✈ *ADD 50% TO 100% PREMIUM FOR FLAWLESS CONDITION WITH TAG*

BEANIE HUNTER'S TIPS: Steg, like his prehistoric buddies Rex and Bronty, is one of the most sought after Beanies. Beanie Hunters on the Internet frequently report that $5 Steg is not extinct in the bins of out-of-the-way gift shops, but we've yet to run into such good luck.

☼ **STING** ☼

(The Manta Ray)

TOTAL MADE:	500,000	Birthday: 8-27-95
(Est.) Survival 2007:	50,000	*Retired:* <u>Dec., 1996</u>

ISSUE PRICE:	**$5.00**
1997 Value	**50.00**
(Est.) Year 2007	**400.00**

 HIGHLY
RECOMMENDED

✈ *ADD 50% TO 100% PREMIUM FOR*
FLAWLESS CONDITION WITH TAG

<u>**BEANIE HUNTER'S TIPS:**</u> Occasionally found in smaller gift shops for $5, Sting should be purchased ASAP at up to $50. His tie-dyed fabric matches Bronty's. As we were going to press, we heard of a Beanie Baby dealer who was pleasantly surprised to receive some 250 pieces of the retired Sting at his regular unit cost! (What to do?)

STINKY
(The Skunk)

TOTAL MADE:	2,000,000	Birthday: 2-13-95
(Est.) Survival 2007:	200,000	*Likely to be retired:* **1999**

ISSUE PRICE:	**$5.00**
1997 Value	**5.00**
(Est.) Year 2007	**40.00**

👍 RECOMMENDED

✈ *ADD 10% TO 20% PREMIUM FOR FLAWLESS CONDITION WITH TAG*

BEANIE HUNTER'S TIPS: Heads turn when Stinky enters the room! No, it's not the sweet smell of his plush fabric that commands attention. Stinky is clearly the most beloved member of his breed since Pepe LePew and Odie Colognie! Nevertheless, proper precautions should be taken to avoid pets getting his dander up.

☼ <u>STRIPES</u> ☼
(The Tiger)

TOTAL MADE:	3,000,000	Birthday: 6-11-95
(Est.) Survival 2007:	300,000	*Likely to be retired:* <u>**2002**</u>

ISSUE PRICE:	**$5.00**
1997 Value	**5.00**
(Est.) Year 2007	**40.00**

 RECOMMENDED   ✈ *ADD 10% TO 20% PREMIUM FOR FLAWLESS CONDITION WITH TAG*

<u>BEANIE HUNTER'S TIPS:</u> Introduced in mid-1995 in a darker tone with more closely placed stripes. Stripes the Dark Tiger is valued at $150 and since only 50,000 were made, this price could jump to $750 or higher. The regular issue Stripes is a classic design which captures the imagination of boys (and a lot of girls) everywhere.

☼ **<u>TABASCO</u>** ☼
(The Bull)

TOTAL MADE:	250,000	Birthday: 1995
(Est.) Survival 2007:	25,000	*Retired:* <u>Dec., 1996</u>

ISSUE PRICE:	**$5.00**
1997 Value	**100.00**
(Est.) Year 2007	**500.00**

 HIGHLY
RECOMMENDED

✈ *ADD 50% TO 100% PREMIUM FOR*
FLAWLESS CONDITION WITH TAG

<u>BEANIE HUNTER'S TIPS:</u> Tabasco may have been prematurely retired in order to avoid a legal conflict with Tabasco brand sauce. Tabasco was replaced with Snort (who was apparently assigned the 1995 birthday Tabasco never officially received). Snort differs from Tabasco in that his feet are trimmed in cream.

TANK
(The Armadillo)

| TOTAL MADE: | 2,000,000 | Birthday: 2-22-95 |
| (Est.) Survival 2007: | 200,000 | *Likely to be retired:* **1998** |

ISSUE PRICE:	$5.00
1997 Value	5.00
(Est.) Year 2007	40.00

👍 RECOMMENDED   ✈ *ADD 10% TO 20% PREMIUM FOR*
                              FLAWLESS CONDITION WITH TAG

BEANIE HUNTER'S TIPS: The formidable tank has undergone three style designs. The original armadillo had only 7 bony plates (ribs), whereas the second version had 9. The third and current Tank is smaller, with 9 ribs and a firm shell. Both earlier Tanks are well worth $100 each. Tank shares the same fabric as Spike and Mel.

☼ **TEDDY** ☼

(The "Old Face" Bear)

TOTAL MADE: 50,000 (per color)   **Birthday: 1994**
(Est.) Survival 2007:   **5,000**   *Retired:* <u>**1995**</u>

ISSUE PRICE: **$5.00**
1997 Value   **200.00–600.00**
(Est.) Year 2007 1,000.00–2,500.00

 HIGHLY
    RECOMMENDED

✈ *ADD 50% TO 100% PREMIUM FOR*
FLAWLESS CONDITION WITH TAG

<u>**BEANIE HUNTER'S TIPS:**</u> To date, an even dozen "standard" Teddy Bears (6 Old Face, 6 New Face) has been released in the following colors: Brown, Cranberry, Jade, Magenta, Teal and Violet. In the Old Face group, the original brown Teddy is the rarest, and worth $600. (Magenta is worth $200.) An exciting array!

☼ <u>TEDDY</u> ☼

(The "New Face" Bear)

TOTAL MADE:	3,000,000*	Birthday: 11-28-95
(Est.) Survival 2007:	300,000	*Likely to be retired:* <u>**1997**</u>

ISSUE PRICE:	**$5.00**
1997 Value	**5.00**
(Est.) Year 2007	**40.00**

 RECOMMENDED ✈*ADD 10% TO 20% PREMIUM FOR FLAWLESS CONDITION WITH TAG*

<u>**BEANIE HUNTER'S TIPS:**</u> *The information above applies only to the common Brown Face Teddy. All 5 retired colors (the same colors as Old Face) fall into the $500-$750 price range with an estimated 50,000 of each produced. Highly recommended. There are also 4 "specialty" New Face bears: Curly, Garcia, Libearty and Valentino.

TRAP
(The Mouse)

| TOTAL MADE: | 100,000 | Birthday: 1994 |
| (Est.) Survival 2007: | 10,000 | *Retired:* <u>June, 1995</u> |

ISSUE PRICE:	**$5.00**
1997 Value	**350.00**
(Est.) Year 2007	**1,000.00**

 **HIGHLY
RECOMMENDED**

✈ *ADD 50% TO 100% PREMIUM FOR
FLAWLESS CONDITION WITH TAG*

<u>**BEANIE HUNTER'S TIPS:**</u> Presenting a modest and perhaps uninspiring appearance, quaint little Trap is nonetheless one of the scarcer, most highly collectible Beanies. Many predator Beanies, including cats, dogs and Slither the snake, are a threat to this reclusive rodent. But heavy-handed, active kids will thin his numbers more.

☼ TUSK ☼
(The Walrus)

TOTAL MADE:	500,000	Birthday: 9-18-95
(Est.) Survival 2007:	50,000	*Retired:* <u>Dec., 1996</u>

ISSUE PRICE:	**$5.00**
1997 Value	**75.00**
(Est.) Year 2007	**300.00**

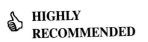 **HIGHLY RECOMMENDED**

✈ *ADD 10% TO 20% PREMIUM FOR FLAWLESS CONDITION WITH TAG*

<u>**BEANIE HUNTER'S TIPS:**</u> Tusk was initially sent to stores with a spelling error on his heart-shaped Ty tag. His name read: "Tuck." Decidedly more intriguing than look-alike Seamore (stop picking on poor Seamore already!), this water-loving walrus is on many want lists.

✪ **TWIGS** ✪
(The Giraffe)

TOTAL MADE:	3,000,000	Birthday: 5-19-95
(Est.) Survival 2007:	300,000	*Likely to be retired:* __1998__

ISSUE PRICE:	$5.00
1997 Value	5.00
(Est.) Year 2007	40.00

 RECOMMENDED   ✈ *ADD 10% TO 20% PREMIUM FOR
FLAWLESS CONDITION WITH TAG*

__BEANIE HUNTER'S TIPS:__ Although common, Twigs is un-
questionably one of the cutest Beanie Babies made. In fact, he's
a standout in his brightly colored jungle suit. Warning: Giraffes
can reach the leaves of your tallest house plants. Feed Twigs
heartily once or twice a month and fence off your indoor vegetation.

☼ **VALENTINO** ☼
(White Teddy Bear With Red Heart)

TOTAL MADE:	1,000,000	Birthday: 2-14-94
(Est.) Survival 2007:	100,000	*Likely to be retired:* __1998__

ISSUE PRICE:	**$5.00**
1997 Value	**5.00**
(Est.) Year 2007	**75.00**

 **HIGHLY RECOMMENDED**   ✈ *ADD 10% TO 20% PREMIUM FOR FLAWLESS CONDITION WITH TAG*

__BEANIE HUNTER'S TIPS:__ If Valentino is retired before next Valentine's Day, you'll be sorry you missed this $5 bargain. Unlike the historic lover (Rudolph), this Valentino won't love you and leave you. Unless detached, his plush heart belongs to his owner forever. In time, this white-furred bear will become quite scarce in pristine condition.

☼ <u>VELVET</u> ☼
(The Panther)

TOTAL MADE:	1,000,000	**Birthday: 12-16-95**
(Est.) Survival 2007:	100,000	*Likely to be retired:* **2000**

ISSUE PRICE:	**$5.00**
1997 Value	**5.00**
(Est.) Year 2007	**40.00**

 **RECOMMENDED**   ✈*ADD 10% TO 20% PREMIUM FOR FLAWLESS CONDITION WITH TAG*

BEANIE HUNTER'S TIPS: For those on a budget, the all-black Velvet is an economical substitute for the rare all-black Zip the Cat! (Just kidding!) With his keen ability to stalk fast moving prey, Velvet actually makes the perfect watch cat.

☼ WADDLE ☼

(The Penguin)

TOTAL MADE:	2,000,000	Birthday: 12-19-95
(Est.) Survival 2007:	200,000	*Likely to be retired:* **1999**

ISSUE PRICE:	**$5.00**
1997 Value	**5.00**
(Est.) Year 2007	**40.00**

 RECOMMENDED   ✈ *ADD 10% TO 20% PREMIUM FOR FLAWLESS CONDITION WITH TAG*

BEANIE HUNTER'S TIPS: Adorned in an oversize tuxedo and a bright yellow "ring around the collar," Waddle is one debonair Pen-guin! He's the most colorful bird in production, and he knows to keep his distance from Splash and Crunch! A pair of Waddles will dress up a bathroom vanity, a fireplace mantle or a formal dining room table.

☼ **WEB** ☼
(The Spider)

TOTAL MADE:	**100,000**	**Birthday:** 1994	
(Est.) Survival 2007:	**10,000**	*Retired:* <u>**1995**</u>	

ISSUE PRICE:	**$5.00**
1997 Value	**300.00**
(Est.) Year 2007	**2,000.00**

 **HIGHLY RECOMMENDED**

✈ *ADD 50% TO 100% PREMIUM FOR FLAWLESS CONDITION WITH TAG*

BEANIE HUNTER'S TIPS: Since Web is another poemless Beanie, feel free to recite "The Itsy Bitsy Spider" whenever you let him out to stretch his long, lithe legs. (Keep Web away from water spouts!) With a relatively low population to begin with, we're sure that in 10 years there will be few Webs who are not missing legs!

☼ WEENIE ☼
(The Dachshund)

TOTAL MADE:	1,000,000	Birthday: 7-20-95
(Est.) Survival 2007:	100,000	*Likely to be retired:* **2000**

ISSUE PRICE:	$5.00
1997 Value	5.00
(Est.) Year 2007	40.00

 RECOMMENDED   ✈ *ADD 10% TO 20% PREMIUM FOR
FLAWLESS CONDITION WITH TAG*

BEANIE HUNTER'S TIPS: Weenie was a well-trained 6-month old pup when kids began to adopt him in early 1996. Like all of Ty's cuddly canines, this dapper dachshund is one great hot dog to add to your collection.

☼ <u>WRINKLES</u> ☼
(The Bulldog)

TOTAL MADE:	1,000,000	Birthday: 5-1-96
(Est.) Survival 2007:	100,000	*Likely to be retired:* <u>1998</u>

ISSUE PRICE:	**$5.00**
1997 Value	**5.00**
(Est.) Year 2007	**40.00**

 RECOMMENDED ✈ *ADD 10% TO 20% PREMIUM FOR FLAWLESS CONDITION WITH TAG*

BEANIE HUNTER'S TIPS: Don't tell Wrinkles that his breed has recently been declared intellectually challenged. Technically, dogs arenot permitted to attend classes in school. However, you can let Wrinkles tag along in your pocket if he promises to mind his P's and Q's.

☼ ZIGGY ☼

(The Zebra)

TOTAL MADE:	1,000,000	Birthday: 12-24-95
(Est.) Survival 2007:	100,000	*Likely to be retired:* **2001**

ISSUE PRICE:	**$5.00**
1997 Value	**5.00**
(Est.) Year 2007	**40.00**

 RECOMMENDED

✈ *ADD 10% TO 20% PREMIUM FOR*
FLAWLESS CONDITION WITH TAG

BEANIE HUNTER'S TIPS: Sharing his colors with Daisy, Stinky, Splash, Spot and Zip, Ziggy the Zebra and Stripes the Tiger are the only two Beanie Babies with jagged pinstripes. Riddle: What's black and white and sold all over?

ZIP
(The Black Cat)

TOTAL MADE:	**3,000,000**	**Birthday: 3-28-93**
(Est.) Survival 2007:	**300,000**	*Likely to be retired:* **1997**

ISSUE PRICE:	**$5.00**
1997 Value	**5.00**
(Est.) Year 2007	**40.00**

 **RECOMMENDED**
(*See also: NIP)

✈ *ADD 10% TO 20% PREMIUM FOR*
FLAWLESS CONDITION WITH TAG

BEANIE HUNTER'S TIPS: The current ($5) Zip is smaller than the original version*, now worth $200 likely to jump to $1,000. The first of three Zips had a white mug and a white belly. An interim black-pawed Zip enjoyed a very limited run (10,000) and is worth $1,000. We prefer the larger Zip (50,000 made) as few perfect ones exist.

More - 4 - KIDS!

BEANIE BABY CHECKLIST
How many of the 99 Beanie Babies listed below do you have?

❑ ALLY	❑ GRUNT	❑ SCOTTIE
❑ BERNIE	❑ HAPPY	❑ SEAMORE
❑ BESSIE	❑ HIPPITY	❑ SEAWEED
❑ BLACKIE	❑ HOOT	❑ SLITHER*
❑ BONES	❑ HOPPITY	❑ SLY
❑ BONGO	❑ HUMPHREY*	❑ SNIP
❑ BRONTY*	❑ INCH	❑ SNORT
❑ BUBBLES	❑ INKY	❑ SPARKY
❑ BUCKY	❑ KIWI*	❑ SPEEDY
❑ BUMBLE*	❑ LEFTY*	❑ SPIKE
❑ CAW*	❑ LEGS	❑ SPLASH
❑ CHILLY*	❑ LIBEARTY*	❑ SPOOKY
❑ CHOCOLATE	❑ LIZZY	❑ SPOT
❑ CHOPS*	❑ LUCKY	❑ SQUEALER
❑ CONGO	❑ MAGIC	❑ STEG*
❑ CORAL*	❑ MANNY	❑ STING*
❑ CRUNCH	❑ MEL	❑ STINKY
❑ CUBBIE	❑ MYSTIC	❑ STRIPES
❑ CURLY	❑ NIP	❑ TABASCO*
❑ DAISY	❑ NUTS	❑ TANK
❑ DERBY	❑ PATTI	❑ TEDDY (Old)*
❑ DIGGER	❑ PEANUT	❑ TEDDY (New)
❑ DOBY	❑ PEKING*	❑ TRAP*
❑ EARS	❑ PINCHERS	❑ TUSK*
❑ FLASH	❑ PINKY	❑ TWIGS
❑ FLEECE	❑ POUCH	❑ VALENTINO
❑ FLIP	❑ QUACKERS	❑ VELVET
❑ FLOPPITY	❑ RADAR	❑ WADDLE
❑ FLUTTER*	❑ REX*	❑ WEB*
❑ FRECKLES	❑ RIGHTY*	❑ WEENIE
❑ GARCIA	❑ RINGO	❑ WRINKLES
❑ GOLDIE	❑ ROVER	❑ ZIGGY
❑ GRACIE	❑ SCOOP	❑ ZIP

(*Retired)

POEM STUMPERS

* * * * * * * * * * * * * * * *

Ty's Beanie Baby heart tags feature original poetry.

MATCH THESE IMMORTAL VERSES TO 10 CRITTERS.

* * * * * * * * * * * * * * * *

(1) "He often gets stepped on and lets out a yelp!"
(2) "She can somersault in mid-air!"
(3) "It's supposed to be a delectable treat."
(4) "His nose is soft and often crinkles."
(5) "Licorice, gum and peppermint candy."
(6) "Every night he eats animal crackers."
(7) "She's teaching her friend Splash to read too."
(8) "Once upon a time in a land far away."
(9) "Diving fast and diving low."
(10) "Until you realize they're spending your money."

THE FUTURE BEANIE BABY "MATCH GAME"

Which new Beanie Babies would you like to see? Connect each animal in CAPITAL LETTERS to its correct name in Italics. (Answers page 128.) Then write us a letter telling us your favorites. We'll send the results to Ty, Inc. and update you in the next edition of THE BEANIE BABY HANDBOOK. Write to us at: Les and Sue Fox, West Highland Publishing Co., Inc., Box 36, Midland Park, NJ 07432.

WOODPECKER	PEACOCK	GOOSE
STORK	IGUANA	EEL
GOLDEN RETRIEVER	RAT	RAM
ANTEATER	OSTRICH	LLAMA
ROAD RUNNER	ROOSTER	BEAGLE
SCORPION	CHEETAH	REINDEER
TRICERATOPS	EAGLE	POODLE
BARRACUDA	PORCUPINE	BLACK LAB
GROUNDHOG	CROCODILE	WOLF
BOY KANGAROO	BLOODHOUND	HYENA
ARCTIC FOX	COYOTE	MOLE
WOOLY MAMMOTH	CHICK	BABOON
TERRADACTYL	SWORDFISH	CLAM
Punch	*February*	*Archie*
Pointy	*Sawdust*	*Eggs*
S.D.	*Bugs*	*Growl*
Howl	*Tunnel*	*Sprint*
Antlers	*Tarzan*	*Colors*
Lucy	*Chuckles*	*Dirty*
Harley	*Needles*	*Doodle*
Fluffy	*Midnight*	*Iggy*
Sam	*Slip*	*Sniff*
Teeth	*Blondie*	*Ice*
Hugo	*Horns*	*Pal*
Cuddles	*Tara*	*Kick*
Snap	*Pearl*	*Shield*

THE ANSWER PAGE

SOLUTION TO MATCH GAME

Antlers/Reindeer	Harley/Roadrunner	Punch/Kangaroo
Archie/Scorpion	Horns/Ram	Sam/Eagle
Blondie/Retriever	Howl/Coyote	Sawdust/Woodpecker
Bugs/Anteater	Hugo/Mammoth	Shield/Triceratops
Chuckles/Hyena	Ice/Arctic Fox	Slip/Eel
Colors/Peacock	Iggy/Iguana	Snap/Crocodile
Cuddles/Llama	Kick/Ostrich	Sniff/Bloodhound
Dirty/Rat	Lucy/Goose	S.D./Stork
Doodle/Rooster	Midnight/Black Lab	Sprint/Cheetah
Eggs/Chick	Needles/Porcupine	Tara/Terradactyl
Feb./Groundhog	Pal/Beagle	Tarzan/Baboon
Fluffy/Poodle	Pearl/Clam	Teeth/Barracuda
Growl/Wolf	Pointy/Swordfish	Tunnel/Mole

PROFESSOR BEANIE'S QUIZ

(1) Manny/Manatee
(2) Nine
(3) Mystic
(4) Flip/Snip/Nip/Zip
(5) Pouch & Patti
(6) Spooky The Ghost
(7) Lefty, Righty & Libearty
(8) Choc., Curly, Ears, Legs, Squealer, Quackers
(9) 33 - Count 'em!
(10) Bronty, Coral, Garcia, Flutter, Lizzy, Rex, Steg & Sting
(11) "Radar" the Bat
(12) See Page 20 (Chops Retired)

POEM STUMPERS

(1) SPARKY
(2) FLIP
(3) SEAWEED
(4) WRINKLES
(5) CHOCOLATE
(6) QUACKERS
(7) FLASH
(8) MYSTIC
(9) SCOOP
(10) LEFTY & RIGHTY

AMAZING BEANIE FACT!!!

Stretched end-to-end, all of the Beanie Babies sold to date (not including the Teenies) would circumnavigate the entire 24,000 miles of the earth!

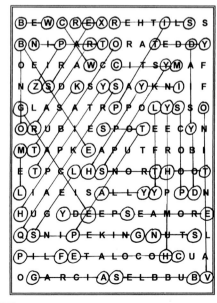